View from the Pulpit

View from the Pulpit

by

Judah Cahn

KTAV PUBLISHING HOUSE, INC.
1982

Library of Congress Cataloging in Publication Data

Cahn, Judah.
View from the pulpit.

1. Sermons, American—Jewish authors. 2. Sermons, Jewish—United States. I. Title.
BM740.2.C33 296.4'2 81-23673
ISBN 0-87068-765-4 AACR2

Manufactured in the United States of America

To My Beloved Wife Evelyn
Truly "A Woman of Valor"

Contents

Introduction ix
A Martian Reports 1
Tensiontown 9
The Poison of Prejudice 24
Academic Integrity 28
Mass Media 39
Political Problems and Scapegoats 50
Politics and Business 65
The Church 73
"The Death of God" 86
The State of Israel—The Faith of Israel: What Is the Relationship? 93
The New Anti-Semitism 99
Is an American Dictatorship Possible? 103
Church and State in Israel 108
Will Israel Succumb to "Exile Psychology"? 117
Peoplehood and Demography 122
A Black Market in Coffins: Did Hitler Really Win? 130
The United Nations Is Thirty-six Years Old . . . Old . . . Old 135
The Thirty-Million-Dollar "Gate" 139
Maybe We Need "Truth in Living" Too! 144
The Czars Are Laughing 149
The Jewish Defense League: An Appraisal 154

Acknowledgements

I shall always be grateful for the tireless efforts on my behalf of my brother-in-law, the late Morton Baum, who was the first President of the Metropolitan Synagogue of New York. He set the course for our institution which guides us to this day and helped create the pulpit from which this view was seen.

I wish to acknowledge the "Master Teacher" of our family, my dear wife Evelyn, who in some mysterious fashion found time, strength and patience to teach and lead us after completing her own successful career. She shared the view and helped me understand it.

I especially want to acknowledge with heartfelt thanks the ever-present assistance of my two sons, Dr. Steven Cahn and Dr. Victor Cahn. They made it possible for me to see the view through the eyes of another generation. In truth it was their cajoling, urging and encouragement which brought this book to fruition.

J. C.

Introduction

History is the story of human continuity. All of us are part of this process and the result of it, and each of us in his own way determines the nature of the society in which those who come after us will live.

In a sense, all of us are historians: we have a curiosity about our parents, our ancestors, and the events which helped shape their destinies. Everyone's perspective of history, including that of the professional scholar, depends to a great extent on the direction in which he is looking and what he is looking for.

One cannot function within the religious establishment of our country without participating in other areas of community activity. A religious leader cannot be only an observer. He must feel, listen, speak, judge, and in the end, be judged by his peers as well as by those whose lives he hopes to affect by his many activities.

The chapters which follow represent the result of forty years of my activity as part of that history in the making. I have attempted to teach and be guided by the values which represent my people's greatest contributions to the history of civilization.

The reader who is looking for conventional literary unity will not find it in this book. The chapters range, as do living experiences themselves, from activity to activity, from problem to problem. The purpose of this book is not to present a theory or construct one. I am not a social or behavioral scientist. Nevertheless, my observations have made me recognize that the best of legislated social reforms will perhaps force people to change some of their behavior and practices, but not their sense of values. I believe man is or can be rational; especially when the paradoxes which exist in our society are called to his attention. And so this book intends to do just that.

The style of the book is more that of talking to the reader than of writing to him. I have refrained from utilizing professional jargon. Most of what I say is based upon observations resulting from my personal participation in the events discussed. The book describes people and institutions in relation to the irrational and illogical beliefs caused by their prejudices.

The institutions referred to are not attacked, but rather analyzed so that perhaps corrective steps can be taken by those within these institutions, and hopefully by those who read this book.

The design of the book is much like that of a picture without a border. The topics I discuss overlap each other, and this is exactly what the turmoil is about. Man cannot arrange his life so that each area fits into a neat cubbyhole—capable of being examined without reference to anything else. We are not merely the sum total of our activities but the result of the interrelationships between the many areas of our lives. I have not placed a border around the pictures I have drawn, because I believe that there is no limit to the expansion of man's potential for greatness, if he is so minded. It is in this spirit of ethical optimism, therefore, that I place my book in your hands.

A Martian Reports

Let us imagine that there is a civilization on the planet Mars and, through some scientific breakthrough or accident, a creature from Mars came down and visited our Earth. Just as we would expect a report of an explorer from Earth who visited Mars, so the explorer from Mars, upon his return to his planet, would be asked to report to his superiors concerning life on our planet. Obviously, the Martian's observations would possess none of the prejudices that we on Earth have, and therefore he would be able to examine our people, our habits, our mores, our morality, our techniques, in an objective fashion. Of course, such a report would be enormous in its complexity and content. However, I can only deal with a certain number of problems in this book, and therefore I should like to limit this imagined report to some of the topics with which I myself will deal later on. The report follows:

Fellow Martians:

My visit to the planet Earth was a most interesting experience. We know, of course, that it is inhabited by living creatures, and we have observed some of their handiwork in the shape of flying machines that circle about the Earth.

The planet Earth possesses many elements. Among them are two which are on its surface: water and land. The greater portion of the Earth is covered by water.

Despite the fact that over two-thirds of the Earth's surface is covered by water, and notwithstanding the great ingenuity of the Earth people, there are still vast portions of this planet that suffer from a lack of water. The Earth people, after all of these thousands of years, have not yet found a method to use most of their water for the primary purpose of drinking, which is essential to their continued life. These people have made some astounding discoveries about energy and matter, but they have not yet been able to use their unlimited supply of water to alleviate the serious water shortage which plagues almost every country on the Earth. On the contrary, they continue to contaminate the drinkable water, so that it cannot be consumed and cannot support the sea life which is a great source of food for the Earthlings.

This brings me to another discovery which I made on my travels. Though no one group of Earthlings claims the distinction of having created the Earth, or of actually owning it, the Earth's surface is apportioned in a peculiar fashion. Separate groups of individuals, each one bearing a different name, lay claim to definite portions. They set up what are termed "boundaries" and maintain their authority over that particular portion of the Earth's surface which lies within the boundaries that have been thus established.

I tried to discover whether there was a rationale to the apportionment of these sections. But there seemed to be no logical basis for such divisions. Some of these places, which are called "nations" or "countries," are so crowded that they cannot possibly support the people who live there. But despite the crowding and suffering which results, the inhabitants are not permitted to go beyond the imaginary boundary lines.

On the other hand, there are vast tracts of land governed by other groups that are so sparsely inhabited that there is a surplus of room. Yet so zealously does each group guard its portion of the Earth's surface that its members are quite ready to kill the members of another group if a boundary line is moved or crossed. I should also point out that men often killed each other in order to establish the original boundaries. Through thousands of years the Earthlings have found no better way to change these lines than by continuing the old method of killing and counter-killing.

In addition to the crazy-quilt division of the Earth's surface, there seems to be an equally irrational division of those things which the Earth produces. Some locations are so poor in the ability to grow things that many who live there are starving. Even if they do not die, diseases strike them with greater force and frequency due to lack of proper food. On the other hand, there are places where so much is produced that it actually costs the people who live there great sums just to store their surplus food. There are affluent countries on the Earth's surface where it costs as much to store the superfluous food as it would cost to feed the starving peoples who live in needy countries. I was quite puzzled by this situation but could find no adequate explanation.

I would like to turn to another phenomenon that I discovered on the Earth: a strange institution called "religion." Now, although all Earthlings *seem* to know what they mean when they use the word "religion," I must point out that there is no such thing on Earth as *the* religion but rather a variety of religions. Though all share this common name, they certainly do not share common beliefs. I know that you will find it very difficult to believe that the Earthlings actually have fought with each other to the point of physical violence over the question of how their planet was created.

More than two thousand years ago a book was written which the Earthlings call the "Bible." This book is, in reality, a small library written by different men at different times. Among these books there is one which describes the creation of the Earth in a most naive and childlike manner. Though there was no one on Earth when it was created and there was no one on Earth for millions of years following its creation, Earthlings are capable of hating each other because of differences in their descriptions of an event to which there is not a single witness.

In all fairness, I must report that there are great sections of the Earth where other religions offer different explanations concerning the creation of the Earth and of other events that have occurred on the Earth. When I discovered that some of the people believed in one fashion and others in another fashion, I assumed that this lack of conclusive evidence might allow them to tolerate each other. But this, I regret to say, is not true. Each claims possession of the only true story of what happened in past ages.

Many followers of the religions that are based on the Bible also believe in what they refer to as as "God." Though they are magnanimous enough to believe that this God is concerned with the entire universe, including us Martians, they hold the opinion that His real concern is the Earth and its people.

Again, I must point out that not all of the people on Earth believe in a God and certainly not in the same type of God. Many religions on Earth do not possess a God concept. There is one extremely disconcerting, confusing element in this God doctrine, as it is practiced by a great portion of Earthlings. They refer to their God as being "omnipotent," all-powerful. Yet they are quick to destroy anyone who challenges the existence or the might of their omnipotent God. Certainly it is reasonable to believe that if their God is omnipotent He doesn't need mere Earthlings to protect Him. I must confess, however, that when I attempted to raise such questions I was almost physically destroyed, a fate that many Earthlings have suffered when they dared challenge these concepts which are held by so many. I should like to warn any of my fellow Martians who may sometime find themselves in the same situation that the more childlike the concept of God held by an Earthling, the more viciously will he defend it.

Though many of these religions differ in their forms of activity or ritual, they all seem to have one common goal: the ultimate peace of all Earthlings. This word "peace" is a most confusing one, and I am not quite sure that I fully understand it. As best as I could comprehend it, it means that the Earthlings believe that all people should allow each other to live in safety and to enjoy the fruits of their labors and minds. In order to teach how to achieve peace, institutions of many kinds have been created. Some religions call them churches, others temples, synagogues, or shrines. They are located all over the world. I visited many of them. Everywhere I heard the word "peace." I heard many other words, such as "brotherhood," "mercy," and "love." There seemed to be an astounding unanimity in praise of all these virtues.

There was, however, one word used quite frequently that I was able to comprehend least of all. It was the word "humility." Some groups use grand parades and magnificent buildings to denote their humility. I found that they competed with each other as to which was more humble, and were quite arrogant in their claims to humility. This, however, represents only one of the many confusions which I encountered on Earth.

One other aspect of the institution called religion and the ideal referred to as peace seemed to me most confusing. The Earthlings obviously love their religions dearly. Many of them would be willing to die for their beliefs, and many already have. Despite this universal homage to religion and peace, I also found that there was hardly a single country on the face of the Earth whose people, while expressing tremendous love and devotion to the teachings of these religions, did not also spend the largest portion of their country's income for guns, ammunition, and other mechanisms created for the sole purpose of killing each other. There are many groups on Earth, each of which claims that its way is the only one able to achieve true peace. In order to prove this contention they do not hesitate to kill anyone who disagrees. I was truly frightened by the ferocity of the peace-seekers.

A third area of my observations concerns so-called communications. Here Earth people have done wonderful things. They have expended a great deal of energy, intelligence, and material to increase the ability of the various peoples on Earth to communicate with each other. They have created ingenious mechanisms and have gradually tied the entire Earth together in one great communications circuit. If on a clear night you look through the telescopes in our observatories, you can see part of that communications system floating about the Earth in the form of small satellites which, though still quite primitive, are very clever. But despite the increased ability to talk to each other, the Earthlings only seem to say things which antagonize each other. The two greatest nations of the Earth are connected by an extremely complex telephone system which they call a "hot-line." This hot-line is to be used in the event that either or both groups decide to destroy each other. On Earth, there is a kind of etiquette that demands that one nation telephone the other to "communicate" notice of this intended destruction.

I would like to comment on another attitude of the Earthlings that I found puzzling. I noticed that there was a great demand among certain groups of people for utensils, furniture, silverware, and other utilitarian items that had been created by artisans, carpenters, and silversmiths two or three hundred years earlier. There were whole buildings dedicated to the exhibition of such items. I examined many of these articles and found them well constructed, some even artistic. But I also discovered that anyone could have exact replicas made at much less cost. The older items are called "antiques." On Earth there seems to be a premium placed on the age of a material object. The older it is, the more valuable it becomes. There is one exception to this rule: people. The older an Earthling grows, the less valuable he is. This is another of the paradoxes with which the Earth abounds.

Another puzzling concept prevails among these beings. It is a most peculiar theory concerning the differences between peoples of varying degrees of skin pigmentation. People with more pigmentation are sometimes harassed and treated harshly by people with less pigmentation. It should be noted that in this respect the people who believe in the aforementioned Bible are the worst offenders. They become incensed if one questions the truth of their Adam and Eve Bible story, i.e., that two people were the first inhabitants of Earth. It would be reasonable to assume that those who credit this story should be the first to demand that all men and women throughout the world treat each other as brothers and sisters in view of the belief that they came from one father and mother. However, the contrary is the fact. Many of these Bible adherents are the worst offenders and the most difficult to deal with.

I must make reference to one particular idiosyncrasy of the Earth people. The "white" people, those with less skin pigmentation, spend the summer months and frequently some of the wintertime in places where the sun's rays make them as dark as the people with more skin pigmentation whom they dislike. You can find them in many parts of the world covering themselves with strange creams and lotions which permit their white skins to achieve this darker hue more quickly and efficiently. It seems that the artificial acquisition of a dark color is far preferable to the natural inheritance of it.

There are many ideas on Earth worthy of commendation. Following the last attempt to establish peace on Earth, i.e., another outbreak of what the Earthlings term "war," they created an organization which is called the United Nations. There is a building on the side of a river in the Western Hemisphere of Earth, in a city called New York, that houses this organization, to which most of the nations of the Earth send representatives. Certainly, it cannot be denied that the organization was a wonderful idea. The nations that comprise the Earth's population were convinced that war was a futile, stupid, and cruel means of solving differences between them. Through the United Nations the people were not merely trying to eliminate war; they also hoped to eliminate poverty from the world and to bring about a more equitable distribution of the good things which abound on the Earth's surface. You see, they were trying to do something in order to achieve what they call "peace."

Many years have passed since that organization was created, and the events and horrors which prompted the creation of the United Nations are still fresh in the minds of the peoples of the Earth. Nevertheless, the organization is now almost moribund. Instead of achieving peace, the rostrum of that organization is used by nations to berate, to threaten, to deride each other, and even to advocate mutual destruction.

I cannot conclude this report without informing you that there were and are many Earth people who see the situation in its correct light. In almost every generation of the Earth's history men arose who tried to point out the prevalent errors and to redirect some of the genius which these humans undoubtedly possess. At times their voices were heeded—but never for long.

In conclusion, I should like to make very clear that the Earth people seem to possess great potential. They are extremely intelligent and capable of many wonderful achievements. They have already accomplished many magnificent things. Some of their achievements challenge even the scientific advances of our own people here on Mars. They have an ability to reason, to create, and to discover. If someday they learn how to harness and channel the tremendous energies they possess, you can be quite sure that there will be no limit to their progress and growth.

Tensiontown

Thirty-five years ago, Tensiontown was a beautiful suburban community on Long Island.* It was made up of a small number of large estates, some of which stretched over hundreds of acres. Almost every one of them possessed a large manor house, one or two guest cottages, formal gardens, a private tennis court, and often what was then a very uncommon luxury, a private swimming pool. It was not unusual for one of these estates to employ a staff of thirty people, including housemen, cooks, maids, gardeners, and part-time assistants. Many of those employed lived on the estate.

In addition to these great estates, the community also possessed a number of so-called luxury homes, owned by those who were wealthy but not in the class of the estate owners. Other homes were owned by professional people, white-collar workers, and tradespeople in the community. These ranged from the almost luxurious to the old and rather shabby. The last-mentioned formed a buffer zone between the better homes and the poorest area of the community, where a few black and Italian families lived. This arrangement was the result of the natural growth pattern of the community. Many of the poorer people worked on the estates as day workers or assistants to the gardeners. They did the menial work in the community and formed the bulk of the help utilized by the various groups in Tensiontown.

The Republican Party was the political power in the community. A Democratic Party organization existed but was of no significance. The town's political posts were held by Protestant Anglo-Saxons who were re-elected year after year. The same men, or at least members of the same families, all of whom had

*The narrative in this chapter, about "Tensiontown, U.S.A.," combines the problems of three actual communities with which I was personally involved and of which I can speak with first-hand knowledge.

lived in the community for many years, were elected and re-elected to the various offices in a kind of political musical-chairs game. Occasionally, there occurred an internecine struggle based on some nonpolitical difference in the community, but such struggles never resulted in any major change.

The owners of the estates looked with benign approval on the officeholders who conducted the day-by-day business of the community. In turn, the officeholders treated the landowners with the deepest respect and greatest consideration. Nothing was ever permitted to disturb their comfort and serenity. The modest local tax rate provided sufficient funds for the needs of the community.

The local lawyers, dentists, and doctors were used by everyone except the very wealthy, who attended to such matters in the Big City. Of course, for minor matters, such as a local zoning change necessary to enable one of the large estate owners to build a new greenhouse or a simple case of measles, a local lawyer or doctor was considered adequate. The local practitioners considered it a mark of prestige to be of service to these distinguished residents. However, most of the very wealthy spent their winters in Palm Beach and were abroad very frequently, so that their participation in the life of the community was minimal.

The religious life of the community was orderly and predictable. There was "the Church," which was High Episcopal. The minister of the church was expected to serve on all noncontroversial committees, and in view of the lack of controversy, he served on practically all committees. Because of his position, he had greater access to the ears of the wealthy than any other individual. Therefore, on those occasions when added funds were needed for a particular local project, it was usually the Episcopal minister who made the approach along with one or two other highly respected citizens.

There was a small Roman Catholic congregation in the community, comprised mainly of the staffs of the estates and two or three of the more affluent local builders whose fortunes were rising along with the development of Long Island as a place of refuge from the crowded city. There was no resentment of this Catholic church on the part of the non-Catholics. In fact, the priest was considered a fine and useful man. He could be counted upon to keep the faithful in line and to give public gatherings a tone of "brotherhood."

The non-Catholics would often make sizable contributions to the Catholic church for specific purposes, such as a new organ or, on one grand occasion, the installation of a new set of chimes. As one good Episcopalian explained to me: "It gave you a warm feeling to lie in bed Sunday morning and hear the church bells ring, knowing that you helped put them there."

Oh yes, there was one Jew in the community. He owned the local stationery store. He was a good-natured, popular, but nonparticipating member of the community, though he could be counted upon to contribute to whatever fund-raising drive was taking place in town. He had visited all the large estates in the community—to deliver the daily newspapers. He had a nodding acquaintance with the Episcopal clergyman and on one or two occasions had spoken to him. His relationship with the Catholic priest was much warmer. The priest frequently visited the stationery store and spent some time talking about the news—although the Jewish owner suspected that such visits were more for the purpose of investigating the titles of the books which he kept in his circulating library than to be social.

On occasion, the priest mentioned certain books as being "very poor indeed" for community reading. But it must be said in his behalf that he never made an outright demand either personally or through others that the books be banned from the shelves of the stationery store. The local public library and the small school library didn't need any supervision. They were already as sterile as a hospital operating room.

The local school system was quite adequate. The children of the wealthiest families were sent to private schools. All others sent their children to the local public schools. The curriculum was limited but respectable. Classes were small and teachers and supervisory personnel adequate. The school budget permitted the teachers to live in a kind of genteel poverty, but they were uncomplaining. Almost all of them managed to augment their incomes in one way or another. Some were camp counsellors during the summer. The music teacher gave private instruction in town, and the gym teacher acted as a referee at basketball and football games in neighboring communities. All were greatly admired, deeply respected, and well-loved. In fact, they enjoyed everything in abundance except salary. Of course, if there were a sudden emergency that required additional money, the local bank always considered the schoolteachers in the community excellent credit risks.

* * *

Let us move the clock ahead thirty-five years. The community is now a brawling hotbed of hatred, racial prejudice, lawsuits, and counter-suits, mutual suspicion, and even violence.

What transpired during these years to cause such radical, terrifying changes?

The tragic story began with the sale of one of the largest estates to a real estate development corporation. The sale came as a complete shock and surprise to the other members of the community. The transaction came to light when the real estate operators made inquiries concerning the zoning laws. Soon after there was a picture of the estate in the *New York Times,* along with the news that the purchasers intended to subdivide it into quarter-acre lots and build hundreds of modestly priced homes. The story stated that the project was an attempt to meet the needs of the employees in a new plane factory which had been built a few miles away from the community and, because of the war crisis, was mushrooming at unbelievable speed.

Tensiontown was caught completely unprepared by this announcement. Its citizens had never envisaged such a calamitous event and did not have a zoning law that would prevent the real estate company from implementing the plan. Zoning laws were now passed at an emergency meeting of the local council, but because of the haste with which they were drawn, they were unable to stand the test of an upper court hearing. All of this took a great deal of time and money, and, of course, each succeeding day witnessed a growing tension in the community.

The owners of the other great estates, frightened by the turn of events, began to search for customers. Of course, you do not put a "for sale" sign on a great estate. Such sales are made in brokerage offices in New York City and the results become known only after the entire business is consummated. Frequently, the large estate owners made contributions to the local "Save Our Community" fund while surreptitiously bargaining with prospective purchasers.

Meanwhile, back at the mansion, other events were taking place which were to have an even greater effect on the community. The initial seller was approached by a local committee and asked—with great diffidence, of course—why he had initiated this chain of events that had resulted in potential catastrophe for their beloved community. His answer was a very astute one. He said: "If I had known what that real estate company had in mind, I would never have permitted this to occur. But, you know these Jewish (or Italian, or Irish) real estate operators! You simply cannot trust them. They told me that they were going to build homes in keeping with the tradition of our beautiful town. Foolishly, I trusted them, but they went back on their word."

Now, this was a bald-faced lie. The real estate company that had made the purchase specialized in the building of small homes. However, the answer, though false, diverted the wrath of the local citizenry. Through the alchemy of prejudice the situation could now be blamed on Jews, Italians, Irish, or any other minority group involved in the situation.

The rest of the community was greatly affected by the prospect of the change. The local grocer had enjoyed a very leisurely and profitable business. He now envisaged the coming of supermarkets with their specials and cut-rate policy. Eventually he would have to compete with the supermarkets for the trade of the newcomers and of the less affluent old customers who, until that time, had to pay his prices because of his virtual monopoly.

This same trend of thought was in the minds of the local physicians, pharmacists, and all the others who had gone their accustomed ways for many years, but were now faced with the serious challenge of change and competition.

The local political powers were faced with a serious dilemma. They knew that change was inevitable. Should they fight changes which were going to occur anyway and go down to defeat as local heroes, or should they go along with the changes and perhaps even benefit from them? The new real estate companies were anxious to gain the good will of the local government. If a little foresight, helped by the binoculars of political power, enabled the town leaders to learn which land was for sale, why shouldn't they purchase the land and then resell it to the developers?

Of course, it was not stated quite so simply. With oratorical flourishes and an intensity born of hypocrisy, they pointed out that by controlling the land they could choose the ultimate purchasers, and thus the community would be guaranteed some degree of selectivity. Local meetings were held at which these same political leaders wept over the fact that streets sacred to them through generations, bearing the names of their own families, were now to be overrun by people from Brooklyn and the Bronx. From the manner in which these words were spoken, everyone present knew that they were not expecting more Episcopalians in town.

But the troubles in Tensiontown were still far from ended. The local zoning board, heretofore something of an honorary body, now found itself inundated with requests for changes in local ordinances and for approvals of projected buildings. Those little houses built on quarter-acre sections had been started, finished, and occupied with a speed never before experienced in the history of Tensiontown. The board now received the plans for the building of a two-story garden apartment house, and if the new order of things prevailed, Tensiontown would soon have its first multiple dwelling.

But one morning the mayor of the community received an emergency telephone call from the town clerk. In a voice so hysterical that he might have been announcing the appearance of an enemy U-boat off the local beach, he informed the mayor that the old Livingston mansion had been sold to a group of Jewish residents who lived in the new section and they had filed plans for converting the main house into a synagogue.

Until the subdividing of the estate, the Jewish population in Tensiontown had consisted of one Jew. Other Jewish families had moved into the new homes. Now there was to be a synagogue located right in the midst of Tensiontown. The local zoning board met in an emergency session to which the applicants for the necessary zone change were invited to appear. A "shrewd" Jewish lawyer appeared for the applicants. He presented a "clever brief" in which he pointed out the legality of the application for the proposed use of the building.

The members of the zoning board and other members of the community who were present at the meeting felt most uncomfortable throughout the proceedings. They had never been in one room with so many Jews. The conclusion was a foregone one and the Jewish representation seemed to realize it. The application was denied and the Jews quietly left the room, but not before their lawyer stated that they intended to appeal to a higher court. The higher court reversed the decision, and before many months had passed, the Livingston mansion rang with the sound of Jews at prayer and the voices of Jewish children in the many Livingston bedrooms that had been transformed into spacious classrooms.

It was quite fitting that the story of the miraculous parting of the waters of the Red Sea should be retold in this environment. Jews in the Livingston mansion constituted a miracle of almost the same magnitude.

Among the new residents of Tensiontown were young lawyers, bright, opportunistic, and articulate. They soon realized that they were looked upon as intruders by the older residents. They were not willing to accept this status and proceeded to do something about it. They joined the long-dormant local organization of the Democratic Party, and for the first time in the history of Tensiontown, a real political struggle was in the making. Nominations to office by the Republican Party were no longer tantamount to election. The great gap between the two parties, which had made past elections no more than a formality, soon began to close: the threat to the Republicans was quite real, and on one occasion, in an election to the school board, the opposition actually made inroads.

The old-timers realized that if they wished to continue in power they would have to win adherents among the newcomers. They approached a number of them and offered them opportunities to join in the political life of the old community. Mind you, they did not offer them positions in the highest echelons, but respectable positions that gave real promise of further advancement. Because ambition is the champagne of human emotions, the old-timers managed to break the ranks of the newcomers; but in so doing they created even further confusion.

As if things were not bad enough, a new ingredient was added which compounded the already chaotic situation. Along with the newcomers who occupied the "development homes" had come another group. This group was made-up of Black workers from the nearby factories who were in desperate need of housing because they too felt it was essential to live near their places of employment.

As I mentioned earlier, a group of older houses acted as a kind of buffer between the better section of town and the area occupied by the Black and Italian community. Some of the owners of these old homes found a very lucrative source of income in the desperate plight of the Blacks who were searching for living space. They moved out of their old houses, subdivided them into small apartments, and rented these apartments to the newcomers at rates which could only be concocted by a mixture of greed and need. In addition to the Blacks who worked at the nearby defense factories, other Blacks who worked in the new shopping centers or who assisted local plumbers, carpenters, and building contractors were also looking for living space. Incidentally, the presence of so many Blacks as laborers at building sites was not due to the liberalism of the builders but to the laxity of the unions. When the various trade unions caught up with these out-of-town builders, the number of Black assistants dropped dramatically.

As the number of Blacks increased, the number of houses renting to Blacks also increased, while the number of rooms in each apartment seemed to decrease. Rentals, however, always traveled a one-way street: up. In fact, the whole procedure became such a bonanza that soon companies were formed for the purpose of buying houses that could be put to such use.

These companies used a process known as "blockbusting." This process, which later underwent many refinements, was at that time more blatant because it was not as familiar. It worked along the following lines:

During midmorning, when the man of the house was at work, an agent would call at a home somewhere within a block or two of the already existing Black ghetto. With great gentility and politeness, he would ask whether he had been correctly informed that the house was for sale. This, of course, was the first that the wife had ever heard of the possibility that she was about to move. Her answer, therefore, was in the negative, but not the kind of negative answer you give to a door-to-door peddler. Instead of saying no, it was not for sale, the housewife usually asked what had given him the idea that it was for sale. The answer to this was a well-rehearsed hesitation and appearance of embarrassment. With great reluctance the agent revealed the fact that one of the homes down the street had been sold for the purpose of turning it into a multiple dwelling for Black families.

Now that he had dropped this nugget of news he excused himself for intruding on the housewife's very busy day and departed. Of course, the housewife's immediate reaction was panic. She called her husband, told him of the visit, and repeated the full conversation. Her anxiety and apprehension were easily transmitted through the telephone. But that call was not the only one she made that day. She also called all her neighbors, first to find out which of them had behaved in such a treacherous manner, and second, to inform them of what was taking place. When the culprit could not be discovered, it was the consensus that, naturally, anyone who did that kind of thing would not be willing to admit it.

At any rate, the machinery was set in motion. It did not take long before the real estate agent was called to the house for further conversations or, if that did not happen fast enough, the real estate agent called again on his own initiative. Finally, a low but not outrageously low price was offered for the house, with the warning that if other houses were sold before theirs, this offer could not be maintained. Faced with the possibility that the house next-door might be sold, a house owner usually proved to be very easy prey. Once a single house in any section was sold under these circumstances, the others fell like tenpins.

This state of affairs led to another complication. The number of Black residents in multiple dwellings increased with such speed that, before long, they began to encroach on the new homes which were part of the real estate development that had been the original bone of contention. The new home owners began to show the same antagonism to members of the Black community that had been shown to them a short time before. This added to the existing tension.

Still another ingredient was added to the devil's brew: the domestic labor situation. Within a few miles of Tensiontown loomed the great factories that were the initial cause of the present situation. These factories were willing to pay even their porters seventy and seventy-five dollars a week. Under such circumstances, why should a man be satisfied to mow lawns, tend furnaces, or put up storm windows for $1.25 an hour?

Women, too, were being employed on the factory assembly lines and, therefore, were not willing to wash clothes, clean houses, and do another housewife's work for eight dollars a day. Those who were willing to do domestic work wanted to earn as much as their sisters in the factories. The remaining estates and luxury-home owners began to feel the labor pinch. They found themselves competing with the newcomers for the services of the local domestic labor supply. The white men and women who had previously served the wealthy members of the community of Tensiontown as domestics, gardeners, or general handymen now felt demeaned because their work put them in the same category as the black population. They began to reject the work they had previously performed.

Mutterings about the "damn Niggers" could be heard in every quarter of Tensiontown. Even the newcomers became restive under the circumstances. Many of the newcomers to Tensiontown, who had proclaimed themselves to be political liberals when they first appeared on the scene, began to speak about believing in equality for Blacks, but . . . Many friendships were strained and even broken over the question. The beauty parlors in Tensiontown, of which there were now many, were filled with talk of the impossibility of getting "reliable help."

The effects of these changes were not limited to the Tensiontown locality. One day a new advertisement appeared in the local weekly newspaper. A different type of employment agency for domestics had been established. This agency promised to provide Black maids from the South who had not been "spoiled" by high wages and privileges. These "girls" would work for low pay and could be trained "the way you wanted them trained." Concurrent with the appearance of this advertisement in the Northern press there was a campaign on in small Southern communities to recruit Black girls who were told of the life of luxury and ease that was waiting for them up North. Many of them packed their meager belongings and were brought North on buses or sometimes in the luxury of a day coach.

When they arrived in New York they were taken to an employment office. It was usually a loft with a few partitions which created interview rooms. They were given meal tickets to a local cafeteria and, if necessary, lodging at a cheap hotel in the vicinity. Some of these girls could neither read nor write. Most of them had never passed beyond the fourth grade of a Southern Black school. Many of them had never handled an electric vacuum cleaner or any of the other electrical appliances with which every house in Tensiontown was amply equipped. The employment agency was reimbursed for transportation, food, lodging, and whatever commission had been established for its activities.

Through such a process thousands of rural Southern Black girls were brought to homes throughout the North. In Tensiontown the result of this procedure was quite sad. The only individuals who benefited from the new labor force were the local repairmen. Vacuum cleaners, dishwashers, dryers, electric stoves were put in the hands of girls who had never used anything but manual carpet sweepers or a wringer washing machine. They couldn't dial a telephone number or write a message.

When I asked the owner of one of these agencies for the qualifications he demanded from applicants before he brought them North, his answer was quite simple. He said, "A character reference from the pastor of their church."

If the ladies of Tensiontown had been adequately prepared for such a situation, if they had been warned in advance that they would have to spend six months to a year teaching these girls all the amenities of a contemporary and electrified household, perhaps the situation would not have been quite as bad. But the ladies of Tensiontown wanted immediate assistance and relief from their daily chores, and therefore, the turnover in household help became almost scandalous.

After a month or two, when patience wore out, the young girl was dismissed and became a stranger in a strange part of the country, with no means of support and no one to whom she was responsible or who was responsible for her. Some of them found new employment within the same community and gradually learned to cope with the challenges of the modern household. Others, who were more enterprising, found factory work more to their liking. Many, however, drifted to the city and onto the public welfare rolls—just another side-effect of the social cataclysm that took place in Tensiontown.

Before we leave Tensiontown there is one other element which must be added to make the picture complete. Although all the residents of Tensiontown were feeling the results of these changes, the most difficult position in town was that of the supervisory staff of the local school district. When the school superintendent looked through his window, where once he had seen hundreds of acres of rolling lawn and open country, now he saw hundreds and hundreds of new homes already occupied and acres of land pockmarked by the foundations of new homes. He knew from his experience with the already occupied houses that the unbuilt ones would soon be populated by young families with hundreds and hundreds of children. These were to become his responsibility, though his facilities were totally inadequate to assume the additional burden. What should he do? If he proposed a budget to his school board that would adequately meet the needs of the local residents and to some degree take care of the immediate future, the "local people," who were still numerically and financially powerful in the community, would literally "blow their collective top." Not only was their community being spoiled but now the school superintendent had the effrontery to ask them to pay for the education of the despoilers.

The superintendent who presented a budget of the kind that was needed would not only lose the vote of the community but possibly his position. Therefore, he stood by and witnessed his classes grow in number from a comfortable eighteen and twenty to a crowded thirty, thirty-five, and even forty. He was eventually forced to place part of the system on double-session and to use many other educational makeshifts because of his inadequate facilities. By doing this he quieted the resentment of the older residents, but now the newcomers began to complain about the educational facilities, the lack of space, time, and teachers. When the superintendent presented the next year's budget, which included the additional sums necessitated by the increase in population, the real battle began.

Hardest hit by the school taxes, which were based on land values, were those who occupied the larger homes. The owners of the little houses were hit least and, therefore, were not too concerned with the rise in the tax rate. Then, a brand-new ingredient was thrown into this seething caldron of economic, political, and racial tension, a proposed referendum for the construction of a new school building. The old building, located in the center of town, did not possess enough land to make further construction on that site practical. Where should the new building be erected? The school board, still made up of the older residents of the community, hit upon a very clever idea. Why not build two schools? One would be placed on the side of town farthest away from the newer section and the other in the midst of the newer section. Then the school district could be divided so that the children of the older residents and those who could afford the better homes would go to the one school and the other children would attend the second school.

These plans were announced with fanfare and pride. They were going to give the community two schools rather than one. But a new and discordant note was struck almost immediately. The Black population pointed out that the way the school attendance lines were drawn, almost the entire Black neighborhood would be assigned to one school. This, they claimed, was a form of racial segregation, and they would not tolerate it.

At the open hearings called by the town authorities for the purpose of discussing the new budget and the question of the location of the new school buildings, the lack of any discussion dealing with educational problems was fascinating. Among the issues raised were such questions as which street was to be cleaned first following a snow storm and why the village plow went through the streets occupied by the larger and wealthier homes before it cleared the streets in the newer sections of town. Certainly the newer residents had to get to their jobs a great deal earlier than the others and were completely dependent on self-driven cars. They had neither chauffeurs nor housemen to dig them out.

Another issue raised at the meeting was the question of garbage collections. In the newer sections of town, only that which was placed in regulation containers was collected. The older residents were able to get all kinds of special considerations and assistance.

Another speech dealt with the problems of the police department. Members of the department were charged with showing favoritism to the older residents. Their cars were never ticketed for parking violations and on special occasions, such as weddings, the police actually closed off streets for the convenience of the invited guests of the older residents.

No sooner was the maker of this speech declared out-of-order than another speaker arose to complain that the local fire department, a volunteer unit made up exclusively of older residents, seemed to respond with greater speed to calls from the older section than to those from the newer sections. The meeting ended in total confusion.

More meetings were held. Someone came up with the idea that instead of building two schools they should build three: one in the older section of town, one in the newer section, and one in the Black section. The advocates of this plan suddenly became champions of what they called the "neighborhood school." The concept of the neighborhood school became the Holy Grail, Mecca, and Mount Sinai all rolled into one. The situation was allowed to fester. The results were lawsuits and counter-suits. Issues were no longer important. Compromise and conciliation were practically impossible. What about the children? As each meeting ended in disorder and each school day began, each child was getting less and less space in which he would receive less and less instruction as preparation for a world that was demanding more and more education.

The Poison of Prejudice

The events described in the previous chapter, which seem to be so senseless and violent, must arouse within all of us not only a feeling of revulsion but a sense of puzzlement as to why such things take place. We must begin to ask ourselves just what it is in the human psyche which allows people to become so violent when other human beings cross their paths and possibly frustrate their aims? Why do we resort to violence and terror to achieve our purposes when reason and logic could serve equally as well? To answer this question would necessitate a whole series of books endeavoring to describe the function and purpose of prejudice in our lives. But we can make a few observations.

The first observation I would like to make concerning the anatomy of prejudice is the fact that all beliefs and attitudes are functional in character. Therefore, when we deal with the subject of prejudice we must realize that prejudices actually serve a purpose in the lives of the people who hold them. I have used the word "prejudice" a number of times and naturally I would like to make clear just what I mean by that word. It is not enough to describe a prejudice simply as a preconceived, premature, or unsubstantiated judgment. There are many such judgments which are not prejudices. Basically a prejudice is a judgment which will not be changed even when proof to the contrary is presented.

One purpose of prejudice is to support a feeling of aggression in an individual. This sense of aggression is created by a feeling of frustration and anger. When people are frustrated in their desire to accomplish something, to do something, to enjoy something, they often take out this sense of frustration on something or someone or some group. Sometimes the target of aggression is not even related to the situation at all, but rather is an innocent bystander.

People who lead mobs or who try to create mobs are not

usually the well-to-do, fulfilled, and comfortable people in the community, but rather the "hangers-on," the partially employed, the unemployed who are angry at their lot in life and utilize any situation as an outlet for their own frustration and anger.

A second purpose of prejudice is to make culturally disapproved behavior acceptable. We have had it demonstrated time and time again that within our culture many people have strong impulses of cruelty, greed, sexual aggression, and other such problems. These people are usually forced to repress their feelings because they are afraid of the social repercussions. They have a need to maintain a position in the community or they fear punishment. Now when some individuals are faced with such persistent needs to express anti-social tendencies, they try to create a situation in which the act can no longer be considered base or unsocial. Thus when we sometimes find cruel and inhuman activity being perpetrated by one group on another, the perpetrators offer the excuse that the group being victimized is not the equal of the group doing the persecuting. This is the language the Germans used about the Jews. This is the language that all peoples who attempt to persecute other groups use about those groups. You see, you would not do these things to a member of your own group, but when you do it to a member of another group it doesn't count, he's not a person.

A Black will rape a White because the White is a white pig. The White will rape a Black because a Black isn't the equal of a White but a member of a subspecie. We are always trying to find reasons why base acts are not as bad when perpetrated against outsiders.

Another purpose of prejudice is to help us in a crisis situation which we do not understand. Man finds it necessary to make sense out of any situation which is close to him and involves his way of life, his circumstances, his daily behavior. When his usual stock of beliefs can no longer explain what is happening, he will frequently seek and adopt new beliefs that do. At such times the individual responds to the only interpretation available to him, and so he resorts to beliefs and attitudes of prejudice. In a period of economic crisis, when the small businessman suddenly finds himself in a critical situation, when people see a country so rich in natural resources slump into a depression, vague beliefs about economic principles are no longer adequate. If at such a time people are provided with a concrete explanation that the "international Jew" has created this situation or that it is because of helping other countries that we are broke, they are quick to accept the interpretation.

Historical studies of anti-Semitism have shown a fairly close correlation between periods of social crisis and anti-Semitism. Man always seeks meaning, and he cannot stand ambiguity for too long a time.

Another reason for prejudice is the need for self-regard or conformity. We know that in our culture the need for superiority is a strong and driving one in many individuals. Differences in language, manners, clothing, education, and income mark off one class from another in American society. Individuals who have a strong need for feelings of superiority will frequently attempt to gratify this need by finding other individuals who can be relegated to a lower class and with respect to whom they can feel superior. It is of interest to note that the greatest degree of prejudice, which expresses itself in mob violence, is among the poor or culturally deprived populations.

There are occasions when a man feels an impending calamity. He doesn't know the real reason for it. All he knows is that the loss of his job will demonstrate that he isn't any good. He tries to find an explanation that will enable him to keep his ego alive. He will eventually come to the conclusion that the Blacks are taking his job, or that the unscrupulous actions of a Jew resulted in his dismissal, or that the loose immigration laws are making him suffer. He cannot face his own lack of ability and, like an Archie Bunker, blames everyone else for his own problems.

Another reason for the existence of prejudice is the need for group acceptance. For example, a man who does not initially hold certain prejudices may adopt them in order to be accepted as a member of a firm, a university faculty, the staff of a hospital, a country club, a fraternity, or even a gang. In this case, prejudice serves as a kind of social admissions ticket. Such people say that prejudice is simply a fact of social life. If they wish to behave in "good taste" and not be pointed out as queer or nonconformists, the best thing to do is to avoid going with Italians, or Jews, or Catholics, or Blacks, or any other group which does not stand well with the predominant one.

We are faced with the problem of how to change prejudiced behavior and attitudes. It is not an easy task. It is not enough to try to prove the error in the thinking of the prejudiced person. What we must do is find the need which the prejudice serves and then try to find ways and means of enabling the person to manage without the use of his prejudice. Where poverty exists, prejudice will exist—not because poverty and prejudice go together, but because where there is poverty there is a destruction of ego, and prejudice becomes a way of salvaging some of that ego. If we eliminate poverty, we eliminate the need for such prejudice and therefore we eliminate the prejudice itself. I know this sounds like an oversimplification, and perhaps in a way it is. But if you will understand this as I present it—as a basic outline rather than a total thesis—then it is not an oversimplified panacea, but an indicator of why prejudice exists and how we can best eliminate it.

So long as human beings have egos, so long as they are fearful or frustrated people, prejudice will exist. We must assume this. The only caution we must take is that society must not permit such prejudices to mold or dictate its behavior toward groups and individuals. Whether we are dealing with prejudice of the Christian world against Jews or of Jews against Christians, or the Arab world against Israel, or the Irish against the English, or the North Italian against the Southern Italian, the same elements make up the brew. These are difficult times economically, and because they are, the role of prejudice takes on greater importance. If we are going to combat prejudice, the first thing we must do is try to understand it rationally, objectively. Only then can we escape the panic which prejudices frequently create and seek solutions which are effective.

Academic Integrity

Though the problem of racial integration still haunts our educational system, it is not the only important problem confronting our schools. Hopefully, we shall assume that the moral integrity and intellectual capacity of the majority of the American people will finally enable them to see the necessity for integrated education on a high-quality level, so that they will find and take the necessary steps to achieve this goal. There are many other problems on the educational scene which must be faced and solved before we can be confident that our schools are creating a generation that will aspire to higher moral values than we ourselves possess. In this chapter I would like to deal with those leaders of our people who are among the most negligent and hypocritical.

In the field of so-called higher education, we are dealing with an intellectual "establishment" whose members have the power to direct and instruct the future leaders of our nation. They possess the authority and means to create an intellectual climate in our nation which will have the greatest single influence on the future and nature of American society.

All of us realize that science is placing into our hands greater and greater control of the universe. By virtue of this control, we have been given immense power to destroy each other. Power in itself is amoral, it is neither good nor bad. It becomes good or bad only as it is put to use. Power is the product of science, and science is the product of education. It appears quite obvious, therefore, that the purposes and processes of education are of equal importance.

Education in itself is no guarantee of moral conduct, nor does it inevitably lead to a belief in those values which create a free and dignified society. Some of the Nazi leaders who were responsible for untold human depravity were men of high educational training and achievement. Doctors of medicine, law, and philosophy were to be found among the most ardent supporters of Adolf Hitler. Many other unscrupulous and power-drugged leaders in all other lands, including our own, were and are highly educated individuals. We must face the harsh but real fact that if, in one generation, we can suffer the greatest war in the history of mankind and live under the constant threat of an even greater one, there must exist some fault in our educational system. Hitler, Stalin, Mussolini, Franco, and scores of other major and minor tyrants did not appear on the world scene suddenly and unexpectedly. In addition, many of them outlined quite fully the purposes and methods of their programs long before they achieved power.

Mein Kampf was published before Hitler possessed the power to implement his cruel plans. The Munich pact was not signed by illiterate barbarians but by "cultured gentlemen" who had enjoyed the highest degree of educational opportunities. Some of the people in our own country who counseled the tacit acceptance of Hitler and his publicly stated program of genocide were among those in whom rested our hopes for the future of freedom and democracy. Can we possibly contend that the educational standards and methods that permitted the acceptance and sometimes even the admiration of this immorality should be held blameless for the world-shattering effects which followed? Shall we still permit those same educational values and leaders to govern our thinking, now that man's ability to destroy himself is infinitely greater than it was at that time? Obviously, there must be a change in the goals of our educational procedures.

This is not the first time that such changes in educational values have been needed and sought. In the period preceding the industrial revolution, the educated man was one who had many skills. Thomas Jefferson, for example, could design the beautiful buildings of the University of Virginia, cross-breed potatoes, write a grammar of the Gaelic language, play the violin, write excellent articles on the history of political science, and be politician enough to become president of the United States. Jefferson was not unique. At that time the mark of an educated man was the possession of many and diverse skills.

The industrial revolution changed the entire pattern of living, including the goals of education. Changing demands created different problems. It was no longer sufficient to create a machine. The user had to be able to derive a financial profit. Profit created wealth, and wealth created power.

Wealth and wisdom make an admirable combination, but they are not necessarily bound together or dependent on each other. Power is more apt to be found in the camp of the wealthy than in the camp of the wise. None but a few purists ever refused the gifts of the wealthy because of the source of the wealth. The "robber barons," whose legendary and notorious exploits frequently ruined and destroyed many who trusted them, became the endowers of churches, theological schools, and universities.

The most sagacious university presidents, the most erudite professors were dependent for growth and influence on this great wealth.

The world was no longer a place for amateurs but for highly skilled professionals. As the industrial revolution grew in size and complexity, it issued a call for specialists—men who knew more about one specific field than other men, and whose value to the industrial revolution, thereby, became greater.

These changing demands are reflected on the educational scene. At the college level, courses in the so-called humanities have diminished in number and importance in favor of the sciences. This does not mean that every college changed at the same time, under the same conditions, and to the same degree. But every college did change in some degree and for reasons which we can well understand.

Specialized professional schools assumed greater importance in the educational picture. Within the last twenty years we have witnessed the flowering of this process. The undergraduate school serves more and more as a preparatory department for the professional school. Students in undergraduate schools try to acquire as many credits as possible in specialized fields in order to make their applications to professional schools as strong as possible. Of what use are courses in music, drama, philosophy, when applying to a technical school? As success becomes more and more dependent on specialization, the facilities of the professional schools cannot keep pace with the applications for admission.

Higher and higher standards are used to evaluate the applicants. The undergraduate schools, in turn, must prepare their students with ever growing intensity so that they can meet these higher standards. Such a process requires more courses, more teachers, more equipment. Budgetary problems become acute. The moneys available to the colleges must be apportioned so that the departments which attract the highest enrollment receive the greatest support. Only the most heavily endowed schools can afford the luxury of maintaining a well-staffed classics department.

A marketplace psychology of supply and demand now permeates the college campus. Competition for the services of teachers becomes more intense. Smaller colleges that used to place their emphasis on the relation between professor and students and on the creation of the "well-rounded individual" are now "raided" by the wealthier institutions, and their most able professors are carried off by promises of the higher wages and greater prestige possible in a larger institution.

The annual meetings of academic groups, which at one time were devoted almost exclusively to the reading of papers and the exchange of information, now rival business conventions in their use as a marketplace for manpower.

During the readings of scholarly papers, department heads and applicants alike roam the halls of the hotels in which these meetings are held, hoping for that fortuitous circumstance that will result in mutual advantage. In practically every instance these advantages are material in nature. "Why not?" is the response to this allegation. Is not everyone entitled to earn as much as possible with the talents he possesses? The answer is, of course, he is; but we must also recognize and admit that these are the new values we have placed on academic achievement. These are the values that we transmit to the young people who attend our institutions of learning.

One of the earliest lessons learned by our young people today is that a thing either pays or does not pay. Unfortunately, democracy depends for its success on many things that do not always bring an immediate "pay-off." Moral values often demand sacrifice and unselfishness. The results of such demands may not be seen or recognized immediately, but I believe it is upon these values that the future of our civilization rests.

A few years ago, I listened to a scientist who had participated in the Los Alamos project describe the power of the atomic bomb. He had before him a carefully prepared paper on the subject. About two-thirds through his talk, he began to describe the actual destructive power of the bomb. As he described the havoc which the explosion could create, he seemed to lose contact with both the audience and the paper before him, and though he spoke aloud, he was, in reality, speaking to himself. I shall never forget his final words, words that were not in his prepared text, words he never intended to utter. He said in effect: "I helped to create this monstrous thing. I am one of the people responsible for its existence. But no one has asked me when or how it should be used and I am frightened."

With those words, he turned and went back to his seat. There was no applause, just a hush which indicated that he was not alone in his fear.

The truth of the matter is, however, that if he were asked how to use the bomb, he would not have been prepared to give an answer. This brilliant man is, in reality, a most highly trained technician. He is a theoretical physicist whose intellectual capacity is almost entirely devoted to one highly specialized area. It had never occurred to him that moral problems were connected with his technical achievements.

Our contemporary educational processes have succeeded in giving us a technical competence undreamed of only twenty years ago. They have not succeeded in giving us the moral understanding to use this technology for the peace and benefit of all. There has never been a moment in history when such moral education was more sorely needed.

This is not the only value structure on the American college campus that needs radical change. The complexities of higher education are not limited to changing concepts in the aims and values of subject matter.

One of the most important elements in our world of education is the athletic program that is part of university life. Sports activities have created a new classification of leader: the coach. Athletic coaches are a breed unto themselves. Many of them enjoy a standard of living far beyond even the dreams of a great academician whose achievements have made him a world figure. A coach who can teach his students to win on the football field or basketball court, to paraphrase the Psalmist, can lie down in green pastures and, though he may not enjoy still waters, his cup runneth over.

Coaches are supposed to be the examples of sportsmanship and manhood to the young people of our country. Undoubtedly, there are some who fulfill this function, but many others have contributed to a major breakdown in our educational organization.

During the past few years there have been a number of occasions when we learned of the existence of dishonesty in college athletics. The disclosure of such incidents caused a few heads to wag. More often a shrug of the shoulder or, perhaps, a cynical smile was the result of such disclosures. Our world has grown so callous to stories of corruption, arson, and murder that the moral breakdown of a few college boys pales into insignificance. That is specifically why I have chosen to examine this aspect as part of our story. We have failed not only because of individual acts of dishonesty but because of the nature of the values by which we live and which we teach others.

In order to clarify the problem, let me describe the actual case of a young man who was involved in a situation resulting from this failure. He was blessed with a fine physique and excellent coordination, and enjoyed a great athletic reputation during his high school career. In his senior year, his school coach informed him that he could secure a full scholarship at a particular college. The young man came from a modest home, and the cost of a college education represented a difficult problem for his parents.

A high school coach usually enjoys the same salary as many other members of the faculty, and though he may find it possible to augment his income by refereeing high school and college football and basketball games, his means are generally modest. However, coaches do have a very decided influence on the young men whom they supervise.

When a particular college approached the high school coach in question concerning his star athlete, it was not with the offer of an outright bribe; rather, the coach was informed that his name had been favorably mentioned for refereeing assignments on the college level. Such an offer was both personally flattering and materially beneficial.

Under the pressure of his family's economic situation, his coach's urging, and the very liberal terms of the athletic scholarship, the student entered the college. In his freshman year he discovered that other young men with athletic ability had also been attracted to the college by the same practices. As a result, when these young men became sophomores, the school basketball team achieved national renown. It was invited to participate in tournaments at great arenas such as Madison Square Garden in New York.

Colleges do not send their young men to participate in these contests without the hope of some monetary reward, nor do the promoters of such tournaments arrange them simply to improve the breed of young manhood in America. The colleges receive a generous slice of the admission charges. The promoters take their share. Great sums of money are involved in these events.

But the young basketball player continues to receive the same stipend, which never is enough to do all the things that a young man would like to do.

Though gambling is outlawed in many states, I know that it will hardly come as a shock to reveal that there is a great deal of money wagered on the outcome of these college games. The gambling is carried on by syndicates and betting commissioners who establish a kind of stock exchange dealing in sporting events. They decide the odds that will be offered on each of the games, and they take care of everything which such activities involve. It is a high-powered business.

Paradoxically, a professional gambler is one who tries never to gamble. He avoids gambling in two ways: first, by establishing odds which always favor him, and second, by attempting to arrange things so that the outcome of a contest is predictable, at least to him. The professional gambler hates to take chances.

One day, an emissary from one of these gambling rings approached our young student with a suggestion. On Saturday night his team was to play another outstanding team. He informed the young man that there was a great deal of money being bet on the game. In basketball the betting is not limited simply to the outcome of the game. The bet usually involves the number of points by which the game will be won. Our young man was told that the betting indicated that his college would win by at least twelve points. The student was then made an offer. It was worded quite simply. "We don't want you to throw the game. We don't want you to bring disgrace upon your school by purposely causing the team to lose. But does it make any difference to you or the school whether you win by eight, ten, or thirty points, as long as you win? At the end of the season, if you've won every game by only two points or so, it will still be called an undefeated season, just as if you had won every game by thirty points. Isn't it also true that when your team is enjoying a comfortable lead, your coach sends in substitute players so as not to make the disgrace of the other team and the other coach too great? All we ask of you is that you win the game by fewer than twelve points."

For this little favor they were prepared to give the young man a tax-free gift of fifteen hundred dollars.

This was more money than the young athlete had ever seen at one time. He began to rationalize his position. Everybody was making money on his skill. Promoters, schools, even his old coach was getting "fringe benefits" because of his enrollment at the school—all were benefiting. The college coach was receiving a handsome salary because of the string of victories which the team had achieved. Everyone was getting a share of the pie except him. Under such circumstances it would take a person of great character and moral integrity to withstand the temptation. Unfortunately, average young men of that age, because of the circumstances in which they live and the values which have been demonstrated to them by those whom they consider their models, are sometimes not able to withstand the temptation.

Our young man was no exception. After he accepted the first fifteen hundred dollars, he was less hesitant about accepting similar sums for the same kind of service. The end of the story is not a happy one. Through a series of circumstances which did not directly involve him but were the result of a falling-out among the thieves, the matter was discovered. His scholastic career was ended, and with it went many other dreams.

Where shall we place the blame for this situation? Shall we blame the gamblers who took advantage of him? The promoters who profited from it? The boy who, because of his youth, was susceptible to temptation? All of these are to blame—but, I believe, only in a secondary fashion.

We must place the blame on those who claim to know right from wrong, who teach moral values, but who, by example, demean the values they teach. The blame must lie squarely on the shoulders of the school authorities who permitted this situation to develop. These authorities were the ones who allowed intercollegiate athletics to become big business. It was the school authorities who permitted the alumni association to create a new motto, "It's not how you play the game that counts, but whether you win or lose."

Our universities are supposed to produce the national leaders of our country. We have a right to call upon the educators of our nation to curb the greed of their own colleagues and institutions, to destroy the vicious practices which turn their students into possible pawns of those whose purposes are achieved through corruption. I shed no crocodile tears for young men who sell honor and self-respect for money, but I cannot sit in judgment in the hypocritical fashion of the very people who created the temptation.

An athletic scholarship is a perverted form of the scholarship idea, which was originally created to reward and aid scholastic achievement. Colleges were organized for the purpose of developing the intellectual caliber of our country. Any person who can benefit from an education and wishes to gain it should be given the means of attending school. But to provide scholarships based solely on athletic ability in order to make possible a school's participation in profit-seeking athletic contests is morally wrong. It would be wiser and more honest if a schoool were to run a lottery for its own benefit and permit the public to gamble in a straightforward fashion.

Other college students who participate in fixed games will probably be discovered and bear the brunt of their actions for the rest of their lives. But the college authorities for whom they play and who raise their eyes in pious horror at these goings-on are shameless hypocrites who should be condemned for their activities. Our college students are not simple-minded children. They see and understand what is going on around them. They are not only the witnesses of immorality, they are its victims.

Tuition costs are mounting higher and higher, and the size of classes is growing greater and greater. In some instances, students sit in classrooms before a television receiver and listen to a professor via closed-circuit television. Even as they do this, they are aware that the school authorities have expended thousands of dollars to bring a professional theatrical company to the campus for, perhaps, a dozen performances. The money wasted on one such project would often have been enough to secure for the school a highly competent instructor for a period of ten years.

They see other tremendous sums being expended on attractive, helpful, but hardly essential features of campus life.

We should prepare young men and women to understand contemporary life and cope with the complex choices which it entails. If morality has any meaning at all, it should be the means that enables us to make correct choices in life. Our young people are witnessing the choices which their teachers and leaders are making, but they are not happy or satisfied with those choices. Whether students are correct or incorrect in their judgments, whether we agree or disagree with their methods of expression, we must be happy with their demonstrations of interest and vitality.

Certainly, it is at best an open question whether it is preferable to sit in a classroom and watch a professor via television or to sit in an auditorium and watch an opera or a play. Is the presence of the professor less important than the presence of an actor or a singer? Here again, it is a question of values. I believe that in many instances the choices made by those who conduct the academic life of our community are at least open to question.

I cannot become too angry with young people on college campuses who rebel against authority. I know that some of us become impatient and look upon their activities as a desecration of the values in which we believe. This may well be true. I only suggest that these young people are fighting precisely because they care about something. They would not fight if they felt completely futile or hopeless.

The young people in our world who fight do so because they desire something. It may well be that it is the freedom to make their own mistakes. Our task is to channel this desire for freedom into a constructive process which will bring these young people some degree of self-fulfillment. We cannot be adamant in our refusal to grant their wishes. We cannot ignore their desires. We must be willing to compete with our young people in the arena of ideas. Even if we do not convince them of our way and they do not convince us of theirs, there will exist a mutual understanding and respect which arises between competitors. Their desire to rebel is, in fact, proof of the existence of hope. They are looking for people of integrity to lead them, to encourage them, to protect them as they search for the meaning of existence. But our leaders are lost. They have become entangled in the long, sticky grass of greed, bigness for its own sake, and the striving for a thin veneer of success to cover an inner failure.

Mass Media

Probably the most influential leaders of contemporary society are those who control the communications media. The leaders of these industries—motion pictures, television, radio, and newspapers—not only control the degree and kind of knowledge we possess but also create the images of the people who in time become leaders in other areas of life.

The ability of the media magnates to accomplish these ends and the adroitness with which they manipulate their success have caused many to refer to us as "a nation of sheep." Therefore, the importance of these shepherds cannot be overestimated.

Perhaps the greatest single advance in the growth of the "image-makers" is their increased access to our lives. The ubiquitous "eye" of the television, the transistor radio, and the inexpensive paperback book are now within the reach of all; therefore, the ever increasing importance of those who control these media.

Where can we place responsibility for the moral tone of our society?

That which yesterday was considered immoral, pornographic, and undesirable is today commonplace and accepted. Literature which yesterday was kept out of the country because of its language and plot is now sold in every streetcorner stationery and drug store at moderate prices. The language used in books and plays today is beyond anything that we would have thought possible twenty years ago.

What is the cause of these changes? Is it simply a matter of financial gain? Have authors, publishers, producers discovered or created this rich vein in the American people? Is it that trash is being thrust down the throats of the American community against its will? I do not believe that these are the facts. I am convinced that the hypocrisy and double-standard morality that began on the American scene a long time ago are now coming back to haunt us.

Since the end of World War I, when an unwanted, unworkable prohibition law was foisted on our country, we have developed an attitude of cynicism, paying public homage to certain values but privately scorning them. The morality of the "flapper age" of the twenties was no better or worse than the morality among teenagers today. "Angel dust" and the junkie's needle may be more serious than the hip flask, but this seriousness is due to their different physical results rather than to the kind of morality which created both problems.

Life on the college campus then was very much the same as it is today. The incidents of immoral conduct may not have been as numerous, but even this was due more to fear of consequences than to moral standards. The "pill" has merely changed the extent of activity rather than our values. Perhaps, too, moral standards were more piously praised, but they were just as completely disregarded. Those of us who were aware of the situation knew that someday the truth would out, and that we would no longer be able to avert our eyes from it.

Just a short time ago, I watched a televised biographical sketch of an ex-mayor of the city of New York, James J. Walker. I listened to a speech he delivered before a distinguished and large audience of "good" citizens. This was *following* the disclosures that forced him to resign from his office. Here was a man whose personal and political life was the embodiment of everything that was considered morally wrong on the American scene. Whether he was or was not an actual thief is immaterial. He knew that he was surrounded by thieves. This is a documented fact. It is also known that he was a self-acknowledged adulterer. The applause which followed his introduction and the ovation he received at the end of his speech, all given by substantial citizens, indicated quite clearly that if Jimmy Walker had not been forced to resign, but had decided to run for office again, he would have captured the votes of a very large number of men and women who at that time were the first to decry modern immorality.

Do you think that New York City today is any worse than it was in 1924 or 1928? The gangsters who flouted the law and were turned into semi-heroes by the public; the gang leaders who were welcomed in so-called respectable society; the "speak-easies" and nightclubs which were known to every policeman on the beat but were by virtue of corruption truly "untouchables"—all were part of the "good old days." Is there such a great difference between the violence on our streets today and the terror that pervaded industry in the days when protection had to be purchased from hoods who considered themselves beyond the law and sometimes were? Is the city the present mayor governs worse than the one inherited by La Guardia? All that happens now is that the lid has come loose and some of the stench and filth have spilled over so that we are forced to pay attention. There is not a single kind of pornographic literature purchasable today that could not be purchased then. The difference is in price, not taste. Standards have not changed. What we are witnessing today is a true reflection of the society in which we live and have lived for the last three or four decades.

Perhaps, the shock of seeing conditions as they actually exist will lead us to reexamine our standards. Sweeping the dirt under the carpet will not clean up the situation. Perhaps, we can force newsdealers to dispense with some of the magazines and books that we believe are detrimental to the spiritual and emotional health of young people. The books may thus become a bit more difficult to obtain, therefore, a great deal more expensive, and thus, take on even greater value in the eyes of those who secure them. This will not change the tastes and values of the young people themselves.

Books, magazines, and plays are not to blame for our moral values. We are to blame. We have glamorized so much that should be condemned. We are willing to pay great sums of money to watch and hear men and women whose lives are conducted according to standards that deserve condemnation. We will blacklist a movie star who once belonged to the Communist Party or who seemed to be sympathetic to what were then considered radical causes. But we will pay millions to a movie star whose career has been marked by one immoral escapade after another. This kind of moral double-talk has been going on for years. What do you expect our young people to believe? How do you expect them to react to this hypocrisy? What do you expect them to do?

If this is the manner in which the adult leadership of the world reacts, shall we condemn the men and women who use their talents as writers or producers to hold up the mirror that catches the reflection of our own existence? Should we castigate them because the picture is not a pretty one? The so-called new morality is not really new at all. The only new element is that now we are talking openly about the old morality, and the truth is not very pretty.

If we would like to change the morality that is *reflected,* we must first change the morality that *exists.* Hiding it, covering it, ignoring it will not change it. We have compromised with evil for too long. We have laughed when we should have cried. We have given adulation to those whom we should have demeaned. We have glorified that which should have been condemned.

Is there anything in contemporary literature, on the stage, or in motion pictures that cannot be found abundantly in real life? The answer to this is *no*: and until that answer is changed we shall have to bear the responsibility for the kind of morality that exists among our young people. When the daily newspapers can no longer match fiction in the presentation of morality and dishonesty, then we can begin some kind of moral restoration in the lives of the "emulating generation."

Another handy whipping-boy for those who are quick to blame everyone but themselves for this generation's "flaming youth" is the television industry. The producers and controllers of the television industry deserve no accolades for the trash they spill into the homes of the American public. The brilliant, wonderful presentations sometimes given on television do not excuse what is shown for a greater part of the time. These isolated examples of the excellent serve only to make the condemnation of the trash even harsher than it might otherwise be. We are never quite as disappointed in the average child as in the brilliant child who performs in an average manner. This fact, however, should not induce us to acquiesce when social, political, and religious leaders try to place almost all of the blame for the faults from which our young generation suffers on the shoulders of the television industry.

The rapid development of television as a means of mass communication has, of course, created many problems. As with all other technical advances, our understanding of the social implications has not kept pace with the mechanical improvements. There can be no doubt that television programs do have an effect on society. However, there are more fundamental questions involved. Not every child who watches violence on the screen responds by acting violently himself. A television program may frequently *trigger* an anti-social personality, but I do not believe that television *creates* anti-social personalities.

Even in the programs which feature so much violence, the villains are usually caught or revealed as cowards or cheats. The law-abiding citizen or law-enforcing agencies are usually made to come out favorably, in terms of both ultimate victory and character delineation. Presumably, this too should affect our young people, so that they would want to join in the glorification of those elements in society thus romanticized and idealized. Yet this does not seem to be the case.

Why do the critics of television claim that this medium has engendered an increased degree of moral delinquency? I think the answer to this question is that moral delinquency in our country requires remedies that are neither simple nor inexpensive. Therefore, those who do not wish to face the problem squarely make television the whipping-boy.

But all their efforts will be in vain. They will serve only to delay our coming to grips with the real problems. Our young people today are subjected to a variety of unhealthy forces. Among the underprivileged there exist problems of poor housing and lack of parental supervision due to the need for double incomes earned by two working parents. In addition, our schools do not function to their maximum potential. Special classes, more rooms, and increased afterschool activities with competent supervision are all necessary. True, these all require large sums of money. However, it is certainly less expensive to supervise adolescents in a playground than it is to supervise them in a prison or a reformatory.

Among the privileged families that do not face these problems there exists the problem of the excessive freedom now permitted to young people. For example, at the present time, the only requirements necessary to secure a driving license are physical ones. Driving, however, is more than the mechanical ability to make a car move. It is also the ability to make judgments in terms of where to drive, how to drive, with whom to drive. The ability of children to make judgments has not radically changed over the past few generations. Sophistication is no substitute for judgment. It is merely a coverup for poor judgment. The affluent society is also a competitive society. It is no longer a satisfaction to "keep up with the Joneses." The goal of many is to "keep ahead of the Joneses." The competitive spirit so prevalent among our "better" families includes the accomplishments of their children. In these circles the "deprived" child is one who lacks a privilege or possession enjoyed by his peers. Only "heartless" parents will permit their children to suffer the traumatic injury of such deprivations.

The granting of privileges to children who are incapable of using them wisely is just another result of social competition. To deny a privilege to a child is to admit that other children are more capable, or at least thought to be.

Children are quite aware of this parental competitiveness and have learned how to exploit it thoroughly.

A third factor causing delinquency among our young people today is one I mentioned previously, the actual events described in the daily newspapers. Policemen who are disclosed as thieves, respected community leaders who are indicted for fraud are examples of adult behavior which betrays our roles as leaders. Television at least has the virtue that in most programs the "good guy" wins. Our newspapers tell another story. If only reality could prove the world to be as moral as most television shows.

I do not think that television programs have any real effect on our crime rate. Our crime rate is due to the neglect, shortsightedness, and false economy that our adult leadership exercises in its dealings with young people. It is due to our inability or refusal to deal firmly with those elements within our society which are corrupt and corrupting. If television were off the air completely, the crime rate would still rise if adult society continued to set a poor example. Television shows certainly play a role in reflecting the tone of our moral order, but it is in no way comparable either in strength or in lasting effect to those happenings witnessed by our young people in their day-to-day living, and frequently in their own homes, where principle is sacrificed to opportunism. A healthy society breeds healthy children. We must, therefore, begin the cure of juvenile delinquency by curing adult delinquency.

A unique contribution of our generation to the field of entertainment is known as "sick comedy." The phenomenon of sick comedy has attracted the attention of every segment of our society. Beatniks who relish the blows which sick comedians rain upon humanity, nightclub audiences who have turned sick comedy into a multi-million-dollar industry, and even the intellectuals of our country, who are trying to probe and understand the "social significance" of such comedy, have contributed to its popularity.

The sick comedian is a problem not because he is a rebel but because, in order to maintain his position, he must be a constant rebel, a believer in nothing, and, therefore, the possessor of no values he believes worthy of retention. The sick comedian enlists in an army that is engaged in total rebellion. In other words, though there is much in our society that warrants the exposure characteristic of sick comedy, there is also a great deal in our society that is of value. In his treatment of society the sick comedian cannot acknowledge these values. He loses his perspective and, to use a much-abused term, his "good taste."

The difficulty of defining good taste makes any discussion of the problem subjective. The implications of censorship are raised. I do not think that censorship will solve the problem of the sick comedians, nor will the punishing of one or two of these comedians change the situation. Why a comedian should be put into prison or fined, but the owner of the institution that presented the comedian be allowed to go free, is one of those questions that is never satisfactorily answered.

The fact that these entertainers are so devastating in their humor and are able to see the hypocrisies and contradictions of our society demonstrates a social awareness and intelligence of high order.

These performers know, perhaps better than others, that the people of our country do not possess a single point of view and are not all capable of understanding or appreciating nightclub comedy. Similarly, our national television audiences are made up of people who are not all able to differentiate between truth and caricature. There are great numbers of individuals beset by the very problems that provide the elements of truth in sick comedy. One merely has to read or attend a meeting of an extremist group to realize the "sickness" of those who hate and who would destroy, if they could, the very freedom which makes possible the self-ridicule of our social order.

The comedian who speaks to a limited group in a nightclub and then appears on a television program where he speaks to millions should recognize the changes in material required by the different audiences. The joke about the Catholic priest or the rabbi, quite harmless when told in the intimacy of a club, becomes grist for the mills of the bigots when given national exposure. The bigot already believes the caricature to be a reality. He believes exaggeration to be the fact. Sick humor, when heard by such individuals, becomes a vicious weapon. The needle becomes a bayonet.

Some of the sick comedians believe that the only cure for our social ills is "shock treatment." It is quite true that a most hypocritical ambivalence between morality as preached and morality as practiced exists in American society. Futile attempts are still made to avoid discussion of natural bodily functions. The synonyms for the word "toilet" would make an extensive list. This attempt to make the natural seem unnatural causes children to write obscene words on walls. They wish to shock the adult world by their possession of knowledge they are not supposed to have or express. But intelligent men and women are not little children, and the use of four-letter words for the purpose of creating shock is no substitute for comedy to evoke laughter. There is a great deal of difference between laughing at an attitude toward vice and making vice a virtue.

Some of our comedians today are among the most brilliant satirists on the American scene. It would be a sad day indeed if any kind of censorship board were created to pass on the materials used to satirize the very society which appoints the censorship board. Those of us who believe in the value of satirical comedy would simply ask comedians to use their material with consideration for the possible reactions in the audience. This is not asking comedians to do anything they do not already do. The life of a comedian depends upon his ability to evoke laughter. He does not hesitate to tailor his material to ensure the greatest amount of laughter from his listeners. Certainly the artist who, by his portrayal of bigots, hopes to fight bigotry does not wish his material to be used to increase the arsenal of the bigot.

Of course, I realize, there are so-called comedians who utilize filth as an excuse for humor and the obscene as a substitute for talent. There is little reason to discuss them. Just as there will always be a market for pornographic pictures, so there will always be an audience for such performers. Pandering will exist as long as there is a market for the products. My plea is directed to those artists who detest charlatans and hypocrites and, through the medium of their gifts as humorists, destroy them with laughter. Their talents and the opportunities to reach millions should be used wisely. The keenness which permits them to dissect society so well should be as sharp in sensing the importance of their own positions of responsibility.

All of this leads us to the complex question of artistic censorship. What should we censor? Who should do the censoring? These are just two of the questions which arise immediately. Within recent years, there has been an increase in the number of motion pictures, books, and plays dealing with subjects heretofore considered taboo. I am of the generation that recalls when smuggling a copy of *Lady Chatterley's Lover* or *Tropic of Cancer* from France or Sweden was considered a daring feat. These books are not even in the same league with those that can be purchased today in the otherwise hygienic environment of a drug store. The motion picture industry in our country has also had to meet the competition of foreign films that achieved fame and fortune by glamorizing some feature of an actress's anatomy.

The stage, or what is called the "living theater," has had for many years a greater freedom in its choice of themes, and most problems of censorship do not apply in the same degree to this medium. It is not considered a mass medium. After all, the average play would have to run for many years to reach even a portion of the audience a popular television program reaches within a single hour. In addition, the number of children who attend most stage productions is quite negligible.

Of course, television possesses the largest audience of all. The taboos now existing in the field of television are not only great in number but highly involved. Here the problem is not only the subject matter but how the subject matter should be treated. Since television is seen within the home, it is available to every age group. It would be a physical impossibility either to monitor all programs or to supervise those who watch the programs.

I do not think there can be any arguments in favor of granting complete license to all media and permitting them to present whatever they wish without any restriction other than their own taste. We know only too well that there are people in all enterprises, including the entertainment world, who would overstep almost any bounds in order to make a profit. There are just so many dollars to be spent on entertainment, and if the money is spent in one place it cannot be spent in another. Therefore, even some who would like to do otherwise feel that, in the interest of their companies, they must cater to the tastes of those who seek the sensational and pay well for it.

Somehow a line must be drawn and the matter must be

determined. Up to now, the problem of censorship has been dealt with in a number of ways. One was to permit the courts to decide what is pornographic and what is artistic. The legal history of public censorship contains many test cases. It should be obvious, however, that a man trained as a legal expert should not be called upon to make artistic judgments. Because this is true, a judge merely attempts to decide whether a book or play falls within the "legal" definition of pornography. We know that one man's pornography is another man's art.

Another popular method of censorship is for each locality to set up a board that passes upon all materials presented within that community. The record of this type of censorship is indeed a sad one. I recall a television program dealing with the subject of censorship. During the course of the program the individuals who were in charge of public censorship in various communications media were asked for comments. The concepts and attitudes they demonstrated were so inferior to the materials being discussed that it was very much as if a housepainter were asked to pass judgment on a Rembrandt painting on the basis of the fact that both used paint in their work.

Religious groups too, have set up their own censorship boards. We have no objection to such religious groups establishing standards for their own constituency. We do, however, reject and resent most vigorously the attempt on the part of sectarian groups to legislate morality for the entire country. Yet in the absence of any other process this has occurred. Most of us forget that social vacuums never exist for any length of time. Someone or some group always steps in to fill a social need, and if the need is not filled intelligently, thoughtfully, artistically, or democratically, then it is the fault of those who have permitted the vacuum to exist.

The process of creating standards is a slow and painstaking one. I am certain of one thing, if the process is to prove successful it must come from within the media and not be foisted upon it.

Political Problems and Scapegoats

No area of American life receives closer scrutiny and more frequent criticism than the political arena. The cynicism concerning politics and politicians is a distressing and unfortunate phenomenon in American life. If the business of government is to move ahead under the guidance of our elected officials, then the men who carry its burden must occupy a special place in our social system. It also means that those who are privileged to serve have a special responsibility.

In no other area does the question of moral values loom so large as in this one.

Hardly a week passes in which the newspapers do not report the wrongdoing of some individual occupying a position of trust, thus removing another brick from the wall of confidence with which we try to protect our democracy. Each incident of this kind is a reminder that we are faced with a very complicated moral problem: what constitutes correct behavior for a public officeholder? It is not enough to condemn, ridicule, or act scandalized when such incidents occur. We should be able to set forth in clear language the standards we believe to be valid, binding, and necessary for those who occupy positions of trust in our government. We should have the right to ask a candidate for public office, no matter how great or small that office may be, whether he subscribes to these standards. Only then have we the right to censure those who do not live up to our standards. If we refuse to clarify the standards we demand, if we leave this vast area of behavior in a kind of gray haze exposed to any personal interpretation and possible abuse, then we have only ourselves to blame when abuses of the public trust take place.

What is the nature of public office in a democracy? In a democracy such as ours, all powers reside in the hands of the people. Because all people cannot participate directly in the process of government, they elect representatives to whom they delegate the authority to speak and act for them. However, when the people delegate these powers they do not relinquish them. Therefore, if they decide that these representatives do not reflect their wishes, they have a right to recall them and choose others. This is what is known as government by the consent of the governed.

Some of our elected officials have been given the right to appoint other officials in the government. These appointments must be ratified by other elected officials in order to establish the fact that the acts of an appointed official are the responsibility not only of the one who appointed him but of all who ratified that appointment. Thus, even when offices are filled by appointment rather than election, the democratic process is not violated.

How is a man affected when he is chosen to fill a public office? What changes if any must take place in his behavior pattern, his concepts of right and wrong, his own rights as a person? We can begin by stating a very obvious and simple fact; namely, when a person becomes a public officeholder he ceases to be a private person. Not only his official life but his private life is of interest and concern to the people. The higher the office, the greater the interest and concern which will be shown.

Is this interest in the life of a public official just morbid curiosity which should be resented? Does the public have the right to pry into the life of a public official and demand explanations even for those acts he claims are personal in character?

When a man is given public office he is given power over his fellow citizens. But the power is given with the specific understanding that it does not belong to him but is delegated to him and must be exercised on behalf of the people who have entrusted him with it. If his activities arouse the suspicion that he is favoring one group of people or one person over another, his effectiveness as a public official is lost. It does not matter whether this favoritism is the result of outright bribery, social contacts, or personal advantage—the results are the same. It is neither fair nor acceptable for any person to assert that friendship with a litigant will not bias his judgment in a matter the litigant may bring before him. No public officeholder should place himself in a position where suspicion of the motivation for his activities is possible.

Does this mean that a public official cannot have a personal social life or maintain personal friendships? Perhaps not altogether, but it is certainly true that his friends must be chosen with great care, as the activities which mark these friendships are always subject to investigation and interpretation by others. One who seeks the privilege of power must also accept the responsibility of making such sacrifices. Public office is a lonely place indeed, but if a man does not recognize and accept this fact then he is neither ready nor able to accept the responsibility of holding public office. This applies as much to men of great wealth as it does to those of modest means.

What does all of this add up to? It means that each man who seeks power delegated by the people must be subjected to careful examination of his motives and possible conflicts of interest. Even if he possesses great wealth he must not demand or expect that his position in private life exempts him from a thorough and objective examination of his public life. He must understand that a personal denial of conflicting interests is insufficient to eliminate cause for suspicion. He must be willing to make public the effects which his public acts may have on his personal fortunes. If he is not willing to accept the responsibility of making such a public statement, he should not accept the privilege of public office.

The power of one man over others is indeed a sacred trust. To control the lives and fortunes of other people can be an intoxicating sensation. Democracy must fear most those people who become drunk with power. The news media of our nation are performing a great and necessary task when they thrust public officials into the spotlight and subject them to public inquiry. Public information enables democracy to survive the destructive efforts of those it erroneously places in authority. That is why those who seek to destroy democracy try first to destroy free news media. We must not resent the efforts of the national news media to pry into the lives of public officeholders.

As President Harry Truman put it, "If you can't stand the heat, get out of the kitchen."

There is a great deal of agitation at the present time for new codes of ethics to govern the conduct of men engaged in public affairs. Such codes have long been needed. We must be uncompromising with those who accept the public trust and then betray that trust. We must be firm in our refusal to allow men and women to occupy public office without revealing or relinquishing their private interests. The decisions dealing with conflicting interests should not be left to them but to the people who placed them in office. Above all, we must cooperate with those who safeguard our interests, and we must protect ourselves, through intelligent use of the ballot, from those who are corrupted by power. By doing this we not only protect the political institutions of democracy, but our example will mold the thoughts of the next generation into whose hands we must place the fruits of our hard-fought and bitterly won victories. That is why in any volume dedicated to a study of those who lead and those who are led, the political arena must be discussed.

I believe that the first issue to be faced in such a discussion is the subject of patriotism itself. When we see the cynical attitude of American citizens toward their government, we must ask the question, Is patriotism dead?

What is patriotism? Certainly it is not mere loyalty to a piece of land. Patriotism, rather, indicates loyalty to the way of life and the system of values that prevail on that piece of land. Patriotism is the willingness to place those values above personal ambition and gain. Which fundamental principles and values make our country worthy of our loyalty? Perhaps more than anything else it is our belief in the value of the individual's life, and the belief that every citizen should possess the same rights as every other citizen despite differences in color, creed, or place of origin.

Patriotism places upon the individual the responsibility of making his own personal fortunes secondary to the welfare of the state. It is on this ground that men are called upon to make personal sacrifices in order to achieve what is called the "common good." Democracy is the people speaking through their elected representatives. Therefore, a democratic government is obliged to achieve the greatest good for the greatest number without destroying the rights of minority groups to express their dissent and to challenge the majority opinion, both by ballot and in the courts.

What is the situation today? The word "patriotism" seems to have lost its effectiveness. We are witnessing the activity of a splintered society in which each group places its own interests above the interests of all others. The intensity and ruthlessness with which each of these groups presses its demands for privilege indicates that patriotism is dead and that in its place there has arisen a self-seeking and self-centered drive which makes us fear for the future of democracy.

I believe that the concept of patriotism has been maligned because of its unchallenged use by groups and individuals who neither understand nor practice it. Patriotism was used to cover up the activities of Senator Joseph McCarthy and continues to be the word veiling the evil of the current rash of right-wing activities in the United States.

The Moral Majority would not have accepted Andrew Jackson into its membership. It would not have accepted Thomas Jefferson. They were both too radical. It would have turned down Abraham Lincoln and all the other great leaders who created American democracy. Their ideas are rejected by the right-wing groups in the United States.

These groups have twisted and tortured the word "patriotism" into meanings that make it unacceptable to men and women who love the democracy upon which our country is founded. The time has come when we must recapture the word and refuse to allow such a magnificent concept to be distorted by the viciousness of petty minds which would destroy the very things our patriotism would defend.

I abhor Communism with all my heart. I abhor it not simply because I have read about Communism but because I have seen it in action. I have seen it not only in the Soviet Union but in the drab and regimented life of Poland, Czechoslovakia, and East Germany. I abhor Communism because in its attempt to level and standardize human life it destroys the privilege of individual differences, the heritage of religious training, and the privacy which is so precious and necessary for intellectual growth.

I have talked with Russian youths and Russian intellectuals, and I was embarrassed for them because they were frightened to speak their minds, frightened to show warmth, friendship, or even curiosity.

I abhor Communism because I have seen what it did to the once-proud democracy of Czechoslovakia. I have seen how the standard of living of a nation could be lowered and the lifeblood of the people and their work siphoned off in a heartless fashion. But, even as I abhor Communism, I abhor the beliefs of men and women in our own country who use the threat of Communism to cover and disguise their own anti-democratic beliefs and actions.

One of the principal planks in Hitler's platform was the statement that he was fighting Communism. Was Hitlerism worse or better than Communism? Can you convince the peoples of Poland, Holland, France, Rumania, Hungary, Yugoslavia, and Greece that Hitler's hordes were less horrible, less destructive than the forces of Communism?

Within our own country there are men and women who use the word Communism as a label they attach to any movement or policy with whose goals they differ. When a hack politician is caught committing dishonest acts, he cries aloud that it is a Communist conspiracy. Racketeers, thieves, unprincipled men and women in every area of life and on all levels attempt to cover their acts by professing to be the victims of a Communist plot.

The attempt to use anti-Communism as an "all-purpose detergent" is an immediate and present danger to all of us. We find ourselves in the position of the boy who cried wolf. When we permit everyone to use the claim of being anti-Communist as a means of serving unprincipled goals, we destroy our ability to recognize that which is truly Communistic and that which is, in fact, anti-Communistic. Communism grows and flourishes in societies where want and corruption deprive the ordinary man of his right to live decently. Communism promises every man the right to vote, and this is the one promise it always keeps. Under Communism, every one votes—once—and that vote puts Communism in power. The promise is thus fulfilled and is seldom repeated except under conditions which guarantee its own success.

There would be no Castro in Cuba today if there had not been a Batista who corrupted and looted the society and economy of Cuba. The danger of Communism in Latin America would not be as imminent as it is today if the soil had not been prepared by the corruption and reaction which seems to pervade an entire continent. When life becomes intolerable, the people of any nation come to the bitter conclusion that anything is better than their present lot and are willing to turn to Communist agents and provocateurs. Then we become fearful and support men or ideas possessing a single if dubious claim; they are fighting Communism.

The fact that their own corruption, their own desecration of the rights of citizens eventually creates new chaos and, therefore real opportunities for Communism either escapes us or we deliberately take the calculated risks. A great government such as ours, which represents not only enormous wealth and power but, of even greater importance, the greatest single force for the freedom and dignity of man, cannot allow itself to be drawn into such a situation. People and governments must not be given our strength and moral support simply because they claim to be against Communism.

It is of equal importance to ask any group to define clearly not merely what it is *against* but what it is *for.* Sometimes, when we want to poke fun at an individual who is afraid to take a stand on any problem, we say of him that "he will come out fearlessly for motherhood." But that statement is no longer quite so funny. How much motherhood? Are they willing to take care of mothers who are too old to take care of themselves or who do not have the good fortune to be taken care of by others? Are they willing to give mothers the right to control the number of children that they will bear?

When certain labor unions in this country speak out against Communism and then use every kind of chicanery, physical violence, and bribery to destroy the rights of their own members, shall we permit them to fly the banner of anti-Communism? When a large corporation tells us about the dangers of Communism and then the government finds it necessary to step in and arrest some of its executives for illegal price-fixing, which is a form of robbing the public, shall we permit them to continue to march under the banner of anti-Communism?

We must conclude that the only acceptable form of anti-Communism is a program that is not only anti-Communistic but also pro-democratic. Anti-Communism is not a detergent which whitewashes evil. We cannot afford to permit ourselves to be lulled into this kind of thinking. Communism is too great a danger and the threat of Communism too imminent to make it the whip with which we drive people into other forms of conformity and fear. We must see through the aims and purposes of those who tell us that in order to unlock the fetters of Communism we must permit ourselves to be locked in by them.

We will, in the end, defeat Communism, but that defeat will come when we fight Communism with greater freedom than Communism offers and when we give men greater dignity than Communism can give. Equally important is the need to free people from the fears and the injustices which are practiced by many groups who are equally guilty with Communism of committing crimes against humanity. It should not be our purpose to exchange the chains of enslavement. It should be our aim, once and for all, to thrust them all off, regardless of whether the chains are anchored in the left or right wall of the prison cell.

Why are we so quick and willing to put the Communist label on one type of organization and activity but so hesitant and sensitive about putting the Fascist label on those groups which deserve it? Why do we have such great concern for the sensibilities of these groups?

Some members of extremist groups claim that they are not anti-Semitic. Personally, I am affronted by such disclaimers. As an American and as a Jew I do not measure anti-American organizations simply by applying the measuring-rod of anti-

Semitism. An anti-American movement which is not anti-Semitic is quite as abhorrent to me as one that is opposed to Jews. Neo-Fascism in this country has hidden itself behind a shield of pseudo-patriotism which is not only false but has made honest patriots reluctant to use the word "patriotism." This reluctance has given neo-Fascist elements a field day. Their use of men in uniform and their blatant misuse of phrases and ideas associated with the American dream of freedom have created a false image of American patriotism which must be rectified.

Any group of Americans demanding a judicial system that is not free in its decisions would destroy the American system of government. Any group that refuses to obey the laws of our courts seeks to overthrow our democracy. Any state which conspires to evade national sovereignty is subversive.

Let us begin our attack on such activities by labeling them with their true content. There are subversive, un-American, Fascist groups in the United States that are quite as dangerous as any Communist group. In fact, they are even more dangerous because they have appropriated the vocabulary of our democracy even as they attempt to destroy the ideas which created that democracy. Patriotism in America is not dead. It simply awaits the freedom to express itself without being identified with neo-Fascists who parade in the guise of patriots.

In order to do this, we must strengthen those elements in our society which in turn strengthen democracy, and we must uncover the true worth of those elements and factors which serve as a divisive force on the American scene.

One of these latter forces, which, in fact, has achieved a high degree of respectability, is what has been called the "Political Three I League" in American politics. The term "Three I League" takes its name from a baseball league which existed in the Midwest during the early part of the twentieth century. The league included teams from Illinois, Indiana, and Iowa. The origin of the Political Three I League was the belief that a political party must always present to the voters what is called a "balanced ticket." That is to say, it must have representation from each of the racial or ethnic groups in the community in order to win the largest possible number of votes. When the term was first used it referred to the Irish, Jewish, and Italian voters. The word "Israel" was used to designate the Jews; hence "Three I League."

Though the constituent members of the original Three I League have changed, the concept of the balanced ticket remains the same. Those who advocate continued use of the balanced ticket rationalize the attempt on the grounds that they are avoiding the multiple-party system which exists in Europe and in other parts of the world. As a matter of fact, this is only partially true.

We have a potential multi-party system in this country which is blocked before any of the interests reach the party level. The chief mechanism used for this purpose is the national political convention. Each national party conducts a convention where candidates for office are selected and the so-called platforms are written. Delegates come to these conventions from every part of the country. The methods of choosing the delegates and the mechanisms of the conventions are highly complex affairs. Various special interests are present, both among the delegates and among the "observers" at all sessions. Labor, wheat farmers, dairy farmers, bankers, miners, oil men, natural gas producers, steel producers, and trucking companies are just a few of the special groups present and represented at the convention. Some groups are not officially represented but still manage to make their voices heard. The delegates from states with large special ethnic interests will see to it that nothing is put into the party platform that is distasteful to these ethnic groups. Religious interests are represented in order that nothing be put into a party platform that runs counter to the interests of a particular church or religious group.

Each party writes a platform to win the applause and votes of as many of these special interests as possible. Even the fact that some of these interests are mutually antagonistic does not prevent party-platform builders from making the attempt to incorporate them in one platform. The art of circumlocution rises to genius level on such occasions.

In addition to the party platform there are other devices used to win the support of special interests. Candidates are chosen with great care. Today, for example, neither party would nominate Thomas Jefferson for the Presidency. First, he was a Deist and no great admirer of any single organized church, and he did not hesitate to express these opinions. This alone would have made him "unavailable," since his views would have antagonized too many people. In addition he was a Virginian. This state no longer represents a great electoral vote. It is preferable to nominate a man from a state with a large electoral vote or from a state which may be carried by the strength of pride in a native son.

In state elections the issues are handled in a similar fashion. As we get to the local level the same principle is used but with greater emphasis on personalities than on issues. A "balanced ticket" in a city election implies that each of the major faiths, ethnic groups, or nationalities in the community has been satisfied. A place is found for as many as possible so as to avoid offending any one group. This fear of offending is due, for the most part, to the two-party system in our country. If a Democrat offends the Italians in the city, the "Italian vote" is not divided among other parties, thus diluting its strength. The group switches to the other party as a bloc and can often affect the entire election. This accounts for the frantic desire on the part of political parties to be "all things to all people."

In defense of the "balanced ticket," politicians point out that it tends to break up bloc voting and thereby creates a more democratic spirit. If Blacks are on both tickets, the Black voters will choose between the two Black candidates and not vote as a bloc. The fallacy of such thinking lies in the fact that voters are thereby forced to choose the *better* candidate instead of being given the privilege of choosing the *best* candidate.

The greatest weakness of democracy lies in its dependence on people who are not too concerned with democracy. We must always remember that democratic government is not a "natural law." The natural way is for the strongest and the most ruthless to govern the weaker. Democracy is an unnatural condition created by men to offset the law of the jungle. Just as the jungle quickly overgrows any man-made clearing when it is uncontrolled, so the law of the jungle quickly overgrows and subdues the clearing we call democracy, if we are not careful and vigilant.

We Americans live with a kind of blind faith that the continuity of American democracy is as inevitable as the laws of nature. Perhaps it is good that we should feel this strong sense of confidence in our government. But even this virtue can be overdone. "Eternal vigilance" does not go hand in hand with overconfidence. Even if a form of government becomes more or less rigid, the scale of values within that form is undergoing constant change.

An essential function of government should be to attract the best minds among its people, especially its younger people, to governmental service. Political ambition for elective office does not constitute the only possibility. Government service also includes the nonelective civil service functions which carry on the day-by-day tasks and give life and meaning to the huge, complex machinery of our government.

I do not think enough consideration has been given to the problem of how to attract young people to such service and, after they are attracted to governmental service, how to keep them there. How can we prevent the best minds and the most highly dedicated individuals from leaving the service of their government and going into private industry? Of course, there are the obvious methods, such as making governmental service financially as remunerative as private industry. Let us assume that this could be done, though, I am afraid, it is quite doubtful. There are other factors involved in government service that make it unattractive and drive out many of our best people.

I believe that one of these is based on a characteristic which, though not solely American, has become so much a part of our mentality that it may be termed a principal characteristic of our nation. We are a people who, whenever anything seems to go wrong, must place the blame on someone. We are always seeking a scapegoat.

It is not uncharacteristic of our people that one of the most widely read tabloid newspapers in the country, in reporting the World Series, places the goat's horns on one player after each game. The player chosen seldom belongs to the winning team. This cruel action fits in with the total picture of our mental process. A player commits an error. That error could be due to innumerable factors beyond his control. The error may have been due to someone's misreading a signal or to the player's doing something against his own better judgment at the directive of his superiors. Despite all this *he* becomes the goat.

The problem with the procedure of "finding the scapegoat" is that it constantly eliminates a discussion of *issues* and causes every problem to be solved in terms of a personality or a group of personalities. We always look for *someone* to take the blame. When we are able to place the blame on the shoulders of an individual or a specific group, we feel that the problem is solved and the issue is then permitted to die.

If we study the great controversies in the history of our nation, we will discover that most of them finally centered on one individual. When the era of McCarthyism made a shambles of public service by destroying the security of public servants, the conditions which created McCarthyism were lost in the glare of the personality of the man whose name became synonymous with the situation. When McCarthy was censured the nation considered the problem solved.

But the problem was not solved at all. The people, the political facts of life, the issues that made the rise of McCarthyism possible by creating the climate in which it flourished did not change. They may remain dormant until a new personality arises to give reinvigorated life to the same issues and to bring about the resurrection of the same conditions. McCarthyism was not a new thing.

We have had other "witch-hunts" throughout our national history. Each time the frightening phenomenon occurred, it seemingly ended with the elimination of the leader. Of course the personality of the leader played a major role, but only insofar as he was able to utilize the mood, fears, prejudices, and ignorance of the people whom he led. Without these ingredients the leaders would be helpless.

We live with a system which permits men to be elected to public office and at the same time represent private interests that are seeking favorable action for special favors. It is this kind of situation which makes it extremely difficult for an "ethics bill" to be passed by a state legislature. The men who are responsible for the machinery of the greatest democracy in the world are reluctant to define the condition we know as a "conflict of interests."

If a scandal results from this situation, the spotlight is focused not on the system but on the individuals who are involved. It is quite true that law courts must try men, not institutions. But such trials mean nothing unless there occurs a subsequent change in policy to prevent the recurrence of similar incidents.

One of our great national problems is that we, as did the ancients, are still piling our sins on a scapegoat and driving him off into the desert. But driving an individual or even a group of individuals into the desert of oblivion, personal disgrace, or prison will not solve the problem. It will be just about as effective in its ability to change matters as was the use of the scapegoat in ancient days. Unfortunately, ineffectiveness is not the only result of this kind of procedure. We not only keep things as they are but we become rather smug in the belief that we have renewed our innocence.

The practice of scapegoating constitutes one of the tragedies in our contemporary life. No one wants to take the responsibility for a decision. "Buck-passing" has been developed to a fine art in all spheres and at every level within those spheres. People are afraid to make decisions because they know that an error will never be examined in the light of all the circumstances. They are afraid that if the decision results in an error, the error will be pinned on them even if the decision was right in the light of the circumstances then prevailing and now seems wrong only because the circumstances were altered or misrepresented. No one wants to be the scapegoat; therefore, no one wants to make a decision.

Yet decisions always have to be made. Therefore, the decision-maker tries to hide by creating some kind of corporate entity or by building a fortress of paper and red tape to protect even the smallest area of responsibility.

The saddest result of this "scapegoat syndrome," at least as far as governmental service is concerned, is the discouraging effect it has on young people who contemplate government service as a career. When the practice of finding a scapegoat occurs in a corporation or in an office, it is unpleasant. It is infinitely worse when a public servant becomes the scapegoat in the eyes of an entire community. Mistakes are reported in headlines, and the scapegoat is identified in large letters. Later apologies and explanations are printed in small type on an inside page.

Politics and Business

Scapegoating is only one aspect of our national psychology which discourages men of ability from entering public service. Another frightening aspect is the lack of dignity and respect to which one is subjected while running for public office. On every side, we hear the moans and groans of the leaders of our country as they talk about the failings and trespasses of the "younger generation." We often complain about the lack of standards of our young people and their utter disregard for the values that are supposedly part of the heritage we bequeath to them. Let us stop for a moment and study the kind of inheritance we are leaving.

No better example can be given than our national elections. Two men strive for the Presidency of the United States, perhaps the most powerful office in the world. One of the two men will occupy that office. Consider the language they use during the campaign. The words "liar," "thief," "hypocrite" all occur with regularity. These words are not spoken by the candidates themselves but by those who are responsible to the candidates for the tone of the campaign.

This kind of behavior can no longer be shrugged away with the statement that "it's all part of the business of politics." That kind of reaction may have been satisfactory in the campaign between Cleveland and Blaine, when the world was a much larger place than it is now, but today we live in a "world society." Even the elections that occur in Albania or Bulgaria have become important news. The election of a President in the United States occupies almost as much space in the newspapers of the foreign press as it does in our own. The nations of the world realize to an extent even greater than we do, that the nature of the man who occupies the position of President of the United States has direct and significant effects on their own national fortunes. They react with complete horror at the lack of self-restraint, the utter ruthlessness with which a presidential campaign is marked. They are not aware that hyperbole is the lowest rung on the verbal ladder of a political orator.

During the recent election the situation became intolerable even for knowledgeable Americans. Aside from the political impact that such campaigns have on a nation, can any of us fathom the effect on the young people of our country? What right have we to ask college students to be restrained in their demonstrations, to be less vituperative in their name-calling, more conservative in their charges, after the spectacle of a presidential campaign? It is all well and good to be sanguine and say, "Don't worry, when the chips are down the American people will unite and be the great nation we should be."

We can keep saying this for just so long, but there will come a time when the fragmentation becomes greater than we thought possible and result in national disaster. We cannot afford to be so sanguine about conditions as they are.

I know that this sounds alarmistic, and you may claim that I am exaggerating, but I deny this. Each day I feel more strongly about the dangers which beset us. The complacency with which the American people view all of this is most frightening. We cannot afford the luxury of such divisiveness much longer.

We are witnessing not only divisiveness between parties but divisiveness within parties. The process has progressed to the point where the ranks of both the Democratic and Republican parties were broken during the last election. Does this mean the emergence of a third party? I do not think anybody can answer that question. At the present time, the results of this divisiveness are not quite as apparent as they might otherwise be. But what will happen if economic conditions deteriorate? What will happen if inflation cannot be controlled, or if we go into any kind of recession and the unemployment rate goes up and business conditions worsen? Then all of the aggravations, all of the tensions, all of the frustrations now hidden below the surface of prosperity will emerge.

The time to operate on the body politic is not when it is sick and close to death, but when it is healthy and capable of standing the shock of the operation. Now is the time to do something about a divided America, and unless our leaders have the foresight, the intelligence, and the will to create a new national unity based on the needs of American democracy, we are in for a sad period in our history.

Many years ago, during a period of national crisis, Abraham Lincoln in an address quoted from Matthew 12:25 and said, "A house divided cannot stand." At that time, he was referring to the deep split between the North and the South, a split which resulted in the Civil War, a conflict of enormous and unprecedented horror. When he made that statement he meant that if a nation does not possess a common ground consisting of common values, common hopes, and common dreams, then despite wealth and power, that nation must eventually suffer. He did not mean that everyone had to think alike. He did not mean that uniformity was to be part of the American scene. Quite to the contrary, he was a man who enjoyed a debate. He was an individual who appreciated the values of democracy and advocated the use of democratic methods in order to solve the most difficult national problems.

It is healthy when Americans disagree politically. I think that progress is made only when different opinions clash and out of that clash comes compromise, adjustment, and eventual understanding. I do not believe in force either to create a uniform opinion or to destroy opposing opinions.

A house divided could not stand in the days of Lincoln. It can stand no better in our own day. What can we do? If every man would make of himself a small island of democracy, that would be the beginning of a new day for all of us. The world depends upon the behavior of nations, and nations depend upon the behavior of individuals. We are those individuals. Every man and woman in our nation must be a living example of what it is we wish to achieve. Even if we do not always approve of the results in terms of our personal wishes, we must be willing to abide by the results of the democratic process. Only an absolute monarch or a political tyrant can make his personal likes and dislikes the law of the land. In our democratic system, no one can force you to like what the majority deems necessary. And no one should prevent you from publicizing your dislike or from persuading others to join you in that opinion.

In a democracy, however, we must obey even the laws we dislike. If the political leaders of our country and those who aspire to political leadership would treat each other with greater dignity, would speak with more restraint, and would conduct the affairs of political competition with their eyes on the dignity of the office, then the citizens of our country would see themselves not as the inhabitants of a frontier town, but as participants in a political system which will have a great deal to say about the future of mankind. We could then create an image for those who follow us influence their behavior pattern and help shape their hopes and goals for the future.

No discussion of the American political system could be complete without some reference to the relationship between politics and business. Seldom if ever, do we find self-corrupting politicians. The existence of corruption always implies the existence of a corrupter. Just as corruption occurs for the purpose of personal gain, so the corrupter seeks personal benefit. Is there any difference between corruption in our day and corruption in any other period of history?

The twentieth century will be identified in history by many characteristics. It was the century which witnessed the discovery of nuclear energy, travel by air, television, and other new forms of communication. It will probably be viewed in historical perspective as one of the greatest eras of discovery in the history of the human race. Even more important than the discoveries themselves are the breakthroughs which they represent. Undoubtedly, our children and grandchildren will live in a world that will consider ours archaic. They will look upon our jet planes with the same good-humored bewilderment with which we look upon the fighter planes of World War I.

In all fields there are so many developments that even a Jules Verne would find it difficult to match in imagination what has already become a reality. Medicine is making great strides not only in the conquest of dread diseases but also in the research made possible by discoveries in the fields of chemistry, physics, and electronics. The secrets of the physical universe are being probed to depths which defy understanding by any but the most learned in the field.

However, for as many centuries as man has been alive and in the foreseeable future, his ability to corrupt and be corrupted has not changed. The causes of corruption may change but that is all. I would hazard the opinion that the number of saints in the twentieth century is no greater than the number of saints in the second century. Nor has the ratio of rogues to saints undergone any profound change.

Most of us view this with discouragement. What is the use of trying to help people, to improve them, when after all people never really change? Now, there is a certain truth to all this. I dare say that in the last three thousand years the physiology of people has not changed. The stone which bruised a man in ancient Judea still bruises a man in contemporary New York. The love which prompted sacrifice in ancient days still prompts it today. Heat and cold, bitter and sweet, night and day have not changed. We still covet because we know the meaning of hunger. The world is still divided between the haves and the have-nots. All the years have not given us thicker skins or bodies which can withstand torture any better than any past generation. What is there, then, about twentieth-century corruption which is different from second-century corruption?

Despite the fact that so much has remained the same, profound changes have occurred in the thinking processes of mankind. Each generation has to live with its own values, and the changes from generation to generation have not always constituted an uninterrupted progression upward. Certainly, no parallel line exists between our technological improvements and our scale of moral values.

How will the twentieth century measure up? After posterity describes the wonders and miracles of our technological advancements, what will be said about us? Will they describe us as the people who gave new meaning to civilization? Will our values be remembered as milestones in man's search for a better world?

I am afraid not. I am afraid that our age has placed greater value on efficiency than on morality. Our age will probably be known only as the age when mankind learned to do certain jobs faster and more profitably than before. Efficiency is the hallmark of our generation.

We have made gods of the methods which help us achieve certain goals, but we have neglected the values which should be the end products of those goals. Corruption in the twentieth century has been marked by the same drive for efficiency as technology. We rationalize political corruption by claiming that the end result is to achieve legitimate goals without going through all the red tape which the legitimate process would entail. All of us have heard the expression, "after all, business is business." That seeming tautology is not a tautology at all. It means that certain practices, mores, and values may be utilized in the process of profit-making that would be unacceptable in other areas. It is a confession that a double-standard of morality exists in our social order. When such double-standards exist no one is ever sure which is to be used at any given time. Thus we end up using whichever seems to serve our purpose best.

Twentieth-century corruption has become an exercise in efficiency, and all of our technological developments will remain simply that—technological, unless we are determined that the values by which we live are equally important as the methods we use. We must learn that means and ends are indivisible and that an evil means cannot bring about a desirable end.

Efficiency is no substitute for morality. But corruption is not the only result of this unholy wedlock between business and politics. Some years ago an English author, Brian Ingles, wrote a book entitled *Private Conscience and Public Morality* in which he discussed the problem of contemporary immorality. The thesis of Mr. Ingles's book was that one group in every social order is in a position to impose a standard on the rest of the society. That group is the upper middle class, or as he termed it, the "um-class." Here in the United States the effect of the behavior of the um-class on the rest of society is, if anything, more profound than it is in England. I believe that the greater degree of influence is due to the fact that in the United States the opportunity to attain um-class status is greater, and therefore its effects are more immediate. This striving for success permeates all of our society. We are out to achieve that near-at-hand success, and whatever standards and values the upper middle class uses to achieve success become acceptable standards and values for the rest of the social order.

I think that this is the pattern of our society today. Until the um-class in the United States is willing to establish and live by a scale of values worthy of American society, the rest of the social order will suffer.

Unfortunately however, the um-class in our country is completely adrift without any of the necessary answers. Is a man immoral because he pads his income tax deductions? Are the parents in a "Dry" town to be condemned for serving liquor to their children? Is it moral to punish dope addicts rather than hospitalize them? Have we as yet expelled a man from a social club or a religious institution for operating slum houses in New York or Chicago? Are we truly shocked by the bribery which takes place even in the highest echelons of government?

This is the failure of the um-class. If a man who is putting up an office building must bribe one department of government to get his plans approved, then bribe a union official to get the work done without stoppage, bribe the government inspectors not to be too hard on him, bribe the policeman on the beat so that the unloading trucks can occupy more space than they legally should, bribe the foreman in the plant of a supplier to get quicker deliveries—if he finds that everywhere and every moment he is called upon to do something which is illegal, how long can he remain sensitive to the commission of illegal acts? How long is it before those who accept bribes become callous to such acceptance and make it part of their expected income?

As a matter of fact, such practices have become what is euphoniously referred to as "honest graft." But no matter what name we give to it, graft is stealing. Someone, somewhere must finally pay the cost of the bribery. The excuse is that the job had to get done. Success is the ultimate end. Can you, therefore, blame those who are aspiring to the ultimate goal of success if they follow the same rules and regulations as those who are already there? What guidepost should be used by those who aspire to success? Obviously, the actions of the successful.

The Church

Even a cursory examination of our contemporary social order would indicate that institutionalized religion plays a minor policy-making role in our society. If a religious institution does have significance in a particular instance, it usually is the result of its political strength rather than its moral teachings. Political strength is the result of its numerical status, not its moral position. Quite true, political parties and candidates make their obeisance to God, churches, synagogues, and the various institutions and men who are connected with them.

Congress and the Senate, as well as state and local legislatures, are opened with prayers that usually address themselves to the "Father of all men." "The Father of all men" has had to suffer through many long speeches and filibusters that attempted to deny some of His children their rights because of skin color or because they came from different rooms in the mansion of the Lord. I could give many examples demonstrating that the formal recognition of religious truth and the actual acceptance of such truth are frequently far removed from each other.

It is a matter of great distress to intelligent and concerned religious leaders that many of the world's greatest minds, now busily engaged in mapping new roads in the heavens and creating the vehicles to travel those roads, are very distant from religious institutions and leadership. Though these men of science are engaged in activities that will greatly affect the future of mankind, they have no working relationship with the religious institutions that are supposed to be directly concerned with the very same problems. Such scientists are not enemies of religion, they simply find religion, as it is presently practiced, irrelevant, immaterial, and incompetent.

Our reaction to such attitudes should not be one of anger or bitterness but a willingness to examine them with candor and determine whether they are justified or not. Are religious institutions shepherds from whom the sheep have wandered, or have the shepherds deserted the sheep?

The unpleasant truth is that religious institutions have lost contact with a vast number of people. Those who would deny this fact point to the struggle for social justice in which church leaders and institutions have played active and vital roles. Though these activities are comparatively recent, we are happy to acknowledge and pay tribute to the courage and moral fervor which prompted this participation. But the point of the matter is that those who are indifferent to religion were the initiators of the struggle. The religious institutions of our country did not provide the leadership. They were, for the most part, only followers in the current social revolution. The Reverend Martin Luther King was the exception, not the rule. Religion and its institutions should not have waited until others provided inspiration and guidance.

If religion seeks relevance and support in our day, it must deal primarily with relations between men. It is only through these relations that it can activate other beliefs of intellectual and spiritual validity. To talk of a belief in God or godliness not expressed or exemplified in social action is meaningless and useless.

Man's understanding of his universe has undergone profound changes in the past two hundred years. Our concepts of an ever-expanding universe and the composition of that universe are only indications of the new directions in which scientific explorations are traveling. Scientists themselves find it difficult to keep abreast of the changes taking place with such rapidity all over the world. The "unbelievable" has become not only believable but expected. Science has discarded the "unknowable" and will only admit to the "at present unknown."

Theology, which once played a major role in the life of mankind, no longer does so, because it consists mainly of attempts to justify old ideas. Man has discovered ways of almost destroying the universe or at least that portion of it upon which mankind dwells. We plan flights to other planets. Science is now capable of actually creating life itself in the laboratory. Secrets of the universe, heretofore thought to be safely hidden and thus endowed with mysterious powers, are being disclosed each day, and the mysteries attached to them are being dissipated.

If the guardians of religious doctrine refuse to admit that, as a result of these disclosures, some of their concepts no longer possess validity, then they must not blame the indifference to religious institutions on anyone but themselves. The man who refuses to question the validity of his ideas in the light of new facts lacks confidence either in himself or in his ideas. There should be no area of knowledge that holds itself inviolate to constant reexamination, including the area of religious belief.

This does not mean that we must jettison ideas simply because of their age. Nor does it mean that we must retain ideas simply for this reason. It does mean that any idea, old or new, should be subjected to constant reevaluation in the light of new knowledge. It may well be that, just as new and wonderful things are being discovered about our old universe, so new truths and new values may be found in old ideas.

This may mean that the religious life of mankind could be thrown into a state of confusion and doubt for a period of time. But this is a good thing. For out of this chaos may come new and greater relevance and interest. Institutionalized religion should realize this. Irrelevancy and indifference are its most feared opponents. Irrelevance causes degeneration. Indifference breeds hypocrisy and cynicism.

Religious institutions should utilize tradition as a road rather than as a fence. Tradition is a way of life that should provide us with the wisdom of past experience. The road that mankind has traveled contained many turns and twists, some of which were quite radical and frightening at the time. But more important than any description of the road is the fact that it was created *by men themselves* for the purpose of making it possible to travel in the direction their intellects dictated. It was not planned by some supernatural architect who thus forced mankind to travel in a direction not of its own choosing.

Religious doctrine should permit itself to be examined, challenged, and even changed without losing its ability to retain intrinsic value. In fact, the more mankind discusses religious doctrine, the more valuable it becomes. This is the nature of a true religious faith.

A specific instance of what I mean is man's discovery of new and vast sources of energy. This discovery was part of the new concept of matter that scientific investigation has given man. We now believe that all matter possesses potential energy which can be released eventually. Thus, because all matter is energy and all energy can be exploded, and because the whole earth is matter, it follows that it is possible to blow up the whole earth.

Does this knowledge affect our understanding of the word "God"? Shall we hold the concept of the author of the Book of Genesis that the rainbow is God's promise that never again will the earth be destroyed? But we know now that the fate of the earth is not only in the hands of God. The destruction of the earth is also in the hands of man.

Does this mean that religion and religious institutions have now lost all relevance and significance? Of course, if religious institutions insist on maintaining the point of view expressed in the Book of Genesis, they obviously can have no relevancy to present reality. But if religious leaders are willing to view the biblical story as *one point* in man's intellectual development and our present state of knowledge as another point, if they are willing to recognize that this earlier conception of God cannot be the conception of God in a nuclear age, then religious thought may prove to be not only relevant but most valuable in man's search for his own salvation. The nuclear age has unlocked new sources of energy, but it has also created new sources of peril to mankind, and we can use all the help we can get. Religion, however, can be of little help to us from the vast distance of irrelevancy.

I am confident that religious faith has a place in our time. I am willing to change, eliminate, and add to the concept and vocabulary of my faith and feel that it will still retain its essence as an evaluating force and provide assistance for mankind.

The church must begin to play a major note in our society if the moral law which it espouses and advocates is to become a reality instead of a pious dream.

Religious institutions must examine national life not simply as an *object* of study but as a reality they themselves helped create. Religious leaders may be forced to assume what to some will be a most humiliating posture, that of the sinner who must acknowledge his errors before he is able to correct them. The willingness of religious institutions to assume this posture will be the first great step toward achieving the position of moral leadership to which they aspire.

Religious leadership is not confined to church institutions or clergymen. It must include all those who profess a belief in the efficacy and value of religious institutions, because it is their material help or the lack of it which will determine the life and strength of religious institutions and their professional leadership.

The churches of every denomination have indicated their awareness of the changing nature of our ideas and processes. From the child in the elementary school who is now studying a new concept in mathematics to the highest educational circles, complexity seems to abound. It is obvious that the physical life of a civilization must be reflected in the moral, emotional, and spiritual life of that civilization. The concepts of right and wrong, black and white give way to shadings of gray.

Complexity is a demanding force on the human mind. When concepts and so-called "truths," which for centuries have been assumed as valid, are challenged, we react as do individuals who try to retrain their bodies to perform in another fashion a task that had been done in one fashion throughout their lives. We are awkward, we often rebel, and sometimes we give way to despair. Yet, if we stick to it long enough we are usually able to make the adjustment with some degree of success. What is true in the mechanical world is true in the world of the intellect. If we are capable of understanding that life must be lived in the light of what is rather than what was or what we wish it would be, we can discover effective solutions to our problems.

It used to be easy to define the terms "religion," "spiritual life," "good life." These terms are no longer simple either in meaning or in implementation. Is there any religion in the world which does not claim to have as its goal the brotherhood of man? What does the word "brotherhood" mean? Does it mean that we are to live together in peace and harmony? Does it mean that we are to share the good things of the earth with some degree of equity? Does it mean that we must not violate the lives and property of others? Does it mean that we must respect the hopes and wishes and ideals of other people?

A case could be made for the fact that it means all of these things. Well, what are the church leaders going to do about it? Are they simply to preach these goals? If this is the "spiritual life," then it is really nothing at all. It becomes a kind of "riding on cloud nine" in which the real people of the world, the "doing" people of the world, are not interested. If men are to live in the state that religion calls "brotherhood," then it is up to religion to exemplify in its own actions what brotherhood actually means.

If religion is a striving for the equality of mankind, then it is necessary for us to stand up and be counted among those who are actively struggling to reach this goal. If there are men in high places who oppose this struggle, the church must declare that such men are opposing not merely a political ideal but a spiritual and religious one. Who is better qualified to stand up and challenge those who would hinder the creation of this state of brotherhood than those who have been teaching its need through the centuries. If the church fails to do this, it cannot expect to be taken seriously by intelligent people.

If dope addiction in our nation today is at its highest level, is not this a spiritual problem that affects the very core of our life? Are not the churches, the synagogues, and the religious leaders involved in the question of how to deal with the unfortunate men and women who have become the victims of one of the most vicious rackets our country has ever known?

To lock the doors and reside in the ivory tower of simple pronouncement and definition is really to do nothing at all, except to become a place of refuge for the old and the weak.

Only when a man can no longer participate actively in the life outside will he find it necessary to come to a house of prayer where nothing is done except to speak of the things outside and to bemoan the sins and faults of the society in which we live.

There are many people in our nation who act as if society has not changed since the nineteenth century. Such people, both in and out of the church, consider religion a performance of ritual in greater or lesser splendor and are convinced that a religious leader should be a man who quotes biblical phrases and bemoans any activity by society which runs contrary to the teachings he believes should be practiced by the world. These same people, however, consider it improper if a clergyman gives active assistance to those who are attempting to live the teachings of the church. We cannot help but sympathize with those men and women in the world of science, philosophy, and psychology who have deserted the churches and synagogues because they found that activists, people who want to do something about the state of things, get little encouragement from those who lead the religious life of the community.

Fortunately things are in a state of change. Religious leaders are making clear to the people who sit in the pews that the world is no longer that simple quiet place which they imagined it was. These religious leaders assert that we cannot fight dope addiction by bemoaning it and we cannot fight political corruption merely by pointing in horror to its existence. The great theological debates now taking place within the church are a sign of such awareness. Perhaps the "Death of God" will result in the "Birth of Godliness."

Many religious leaders in our country are involved deeply with material, political, and sociological activities. They are, in fact, very important elements in those activities. They refuse to isolate themselves from the struggle, they will not dry up on the limb or be lost and forgotten. They do not consider themselves useless or irrelevant. They are now aware, as never before, that if religious leadership is to be meaningful, if it is to be effective, if it is to fulfill its obligations, then it must participate in all areas of activity. The church leaders cannot limit themselves to being the conscience of society. They must also serve as guides by being in the vanguard of social progress. Society is a complex mechanism that needs constant study, reexaminatin, and reevaluation. It is to this purpose that religious institutions must dedicate themselves. Only by such participation in the life of the community can the church serve the people who look to it for leadership.

Certain cautions, however, must be observed by the church. There are times when noted clergymen run for public office. Happily this is not a frequent occurrence. I believe that such an act on the part of a clergyman is ill-advised and, in a real sense, most unfair. A clergyman, by virtue of his position, is both a teacher and a custodian of religious law and tradition. In this position he is permitted to speak with authority on one of the most sensitive areas of human life, theological belief. He has in his power the manipulation of symbols and words with high emotional appeal. Because he is a clergyman, he may use these symbols and words without self-consciousness or fear of the challenge that would be aroused if they were used by a layman. A clergyman has the right to stand in the pulpit of his church and denounce or praise on the basis of his own judgment. But if he uses his religious office and the emotional appeal which cannot be separated from that office to run for a political office under a party label and to enter into the process of political bargaining indigenous to that process, then he is doing a disservice both to his religion and to his government. He is trying to possess the best of both worlds and, as a consequence, he weakens both.

If a clergyman wishes to be a congressman, no one should deny him the attempt to fulfill that wish. Then, however, he should give up the role of minister, and with it the protective covering which permits him to say things from the pulpit with religious authority and to play a role in the life of his people prohibited to his opponents.

Only a charlatan or a fool would claim that, in the political system under which we live, an elected officeholder can possess complete moral independence. When a legislator votes on any question, he is not only casting his vote on that particular question, but by his vote he gives strength to one party or another. Every piece of legislation affects not merely the area of life involved in a particular bill but the entire strength of a political machine. Legislation usually provides for appointive positions and these provide the power of patronage, which is the lifeblood of a political party.

Political parties, like most other human institutions, are neither all good nor all bad. This is a fact of life. The politician depends for strength and effectiveness on his party. Without the backing of his party a man simply becomes a lone voice that is rarely effective, and on such occasions when it does have an effect, it is seldom a lasting one. The elected official, as a practical imperative, must, therefore, accept both the good and the bad in his party. Thus, he frequently gives strength to those elements within his party which may be undesirable, unethical, or immoral. He may do this most reluctantly, but a reluctant vote has the same numerical value as an enthusiastic one.

A clergyman should have as his primary purpose the examination of issues and evaluation of solutions utilizing the measuring-rod of his religious tradition. He should not permit himself to be placed in a position where he must compromise those beliefs. If his beliefs are of such a flexible nature that they will accept, condone, or rationalize evil, then he should not be a clergyman.

This should not prevent a clergyman from serving his government or participating in the governmental process when, because of a particular competence, he is asked to do so. The difference in the two cases is obvious. On the one hand, an appointed official is asked to serve. He accepts his responsibility on condition that the nature and purpose of his service will not compromise his beliefs. When they do, he has the moral right and obligation to resign. On the other hand, when a man runs for an office, he asks people to cast their votes for him instead of someone else. He seeks to undertake the obligation of representing those people whose votes he seeks. To fulfill this obligation effectively, he must participate in the organizational alignment characteristic of the legislative procedure. Party discipline and political success, at least under our system of government, go hand in hand.

The role of minister, especially when he participates directly in the processes of government, should not be self-seeking. All office-holding results in the possession of some degree of power, even if it is limited to sending out mail free of charge. If a man wishes to serve his religious faith as a minister, he should not seek secular power. If he desires secular power, he should not attempt to maintain his position as a religious leader. Secular power in the hands of a clergyman is a complete breakdown of that wall which should exist between Church and State.

The clergymen of this country have played and can play a great role in the maintenance and strengthening of American democracy without possessing the power of public office. Rabbi Stephen S. Wise and Dr. John Haynes Holmes were two such men, within recent memory, who played decisive roles in the political arena and whose efforts were effective because their motives could not be impugned. The elimination of James J. Walker and Tammany Hall from their powerful positions in New York and the success of the late Fiorello H. La Guardia, perhaps the most effective mayor in the history of New York City, were the direct results of efforts made by these two men. At that time, the governor of New York State, the late Franklin Delano Roosevelt, bitterly berated both these courageous clergymen because they had involved themselves in political questions. Though both men were close friends of the governor, their answer to him was unequivocal and strong. Morality and public life *were their business,* and they would not rest until they had achieved the goal of a new administration that promised cleaner government, even if by doing so they displeased a very close and dear friend who was the chief executive of the state.

If either of these clergymen had consented to run for public office on the same issues, the motivation for such activity would have been open to question, and the effectiveness of the crusade would have suffered.

The clergy of our country can serve their communities best by joining the battle, by maintaining the freedom of action they possess when they deal in moral issues and finding the rewards of their victories not in the acquiring of greater personal power but in the creation of a better society.

There is another area in which the church must exercise

great caution. There have been many occasions when religious emotionalism has been used by political opportunists to subvert, for their own selfish purposes, the Constitution's guarantee of religious freedom to all individuals. The most flagrant and recent example of this kind arose because of a suit brought by one individual that resulted in a Supreme Court decision forbidding sectarian prayers in the public schools. The resultant outcry over this ruling was far out of proportion to its importance. Cries of alarm went up on every side. A "godless" Supreme Court was taking God out of the public schools and out of the lives of the community.

In New York State the Commissioner of Education, the late James Allen, issued a ruling that should have settled the problem. He ruled that, although it was against the Constitution to begin a class day with a spoken prayer, yet there was nothing in the decision of the Supreme Court which forbade a moment of silent meditation or prayer at the beginning of the school day. In other words, if a child wished to offer a sectarian prayer he might do so. He might, if he wished, devote those moments to thoughts of a lovely poem. If he felt no emotion or was not moved to any act, his mind could remain utterly blank. Thus, in accordance with this ruling, prayer was permissible but it was to be a private prayer. This did not satisfy the people who wanted prayers in the public schools.

It reminded me very much of the young boy who stood praying very quietly at the side of his father. His father remonstrated with him and said, "Speak louder, I can't hear you."

The boy answered, "But father, I wasn't talking to you."

The people who were not satisfied with the commissioner's ruling found fault with it because the problem of prayer was in reality not the issue at all. The problem of God and prayer was secondary to these crusaders. What they were attempting to do was to control the intellectual life of the community for their own purposes, and they found in the prayer issue a socially acceptable tool to enlist the help of well-meaning but naive people who would unwittingly assist these attempts to achieve their desires.

The most ridiculous and blatant form of this community

action has been the recent creation of banners reading, "In God We Trust" which "the defenders of the faith" insist should be raised on the flagpoles outside of the schools. It reminds one of cheerleaders who stand in front of the crowd waving their arms in order to encourage their team to greater efforts. In this case no one is quite sure which team is being represented, and there is just as much confusion about the goals to be reached.

Unfortunately, this confusion does not deter the cheerleaders. Problems of reason and purpose do not concern them because, basically, they are not religious people. They are willing to make a mockery of both God and religion in the pursuit of their own selfish ends.

It is an interesting and indicative fact that the greatest number of "God's cheerleaders" are to be found in our country in the ranks of the extreme right-wing groups and their fellow travelers. They are intolerant, abusive, and vicious in their treatment of all those who may differ with their point of view.

I hold no brief for the woman in Baltimore who instituted the case that resulted in the Supreme Court decision. But it is highly ironic that when she exercised legal rights guaranteed to her by the Constitution of the United States, those who claimed to be supporting the "Loving God of all men" demonstrated their love of God and man by throwing rocks at her windows and beating up her children. She was hounded out of her birthplace and had to flee to Hawaii, where she lived in continuous fright, her family sick from the abuse suffered at the hands of God's cheerleaders.

There was never a time in the history of our country when religious leaders were more greatly needed to lead us out of moral confusion and awaken us from the spiritual numbness which plagues us.

If they do this with courage and dignity, I believe, they will discover two very encouraging facts.

First, there are countless people in our nation who want to live in a decent country which enjoys high standards of private and public morality. They lack the courage to take the necessary initiative to achieve this but need and will welcome such leadership if it appears.

The second fact is that, morally, the American people have not moved too far away from where they should be. Although there is at the moment a vital difference between moral professions and moral practices, it is not so great that it cannot be spanned by examples of personal courage and dedication such as have already won a place of respect and leadership for so many clergymen in our country.

"The Death of God"

Almost every church and synagogue pulpit today is concerned with the problem epitomized by the question, "Is God dead"? The answer which each minister or rabbi gives to this question is known well in advance of the sermon. Those who depend for their preachment upon the concept of God will continue to claim that He is very much alive, and those who are more humanistic in their approach are privileged to talk otherwise. These discussions are usually so philosophically intricate and theologically speculative that they have little effect, either assuring the listeners that God is still in His heaven and all's well with the world , or ingeniously attempting to find a way of keeping the idea of a deity alive without actually using the traditional word "God."

Many people seem to believe that there is something genuinely new and startling or even daring in this willingness to discuss the existence and nature of God. The truth of the matter is that the discussion has been going on since man first uttered the word "God" and used it as a means of understanding the nature of the world around him. I wish to discuss this subject, not with the goal of settling the question, but rather from an historical point of view, in order to demonstrate that it is neither as daring nor as novel as so many imagine it to be.

The first thing we must realize is that the word "God" in any language did not come out of the heavens nor was it divinely revealed at any time to anyone. It was a concept used by early man to explain phenomena in the world which would otherwise have been a complete mystery to him. As soon as man began to take note of the sun and the moon, the seas, the earth, and other natural phenomena over which he had no control, he sought to establish some means of utilizing them for his own purposes. This is why man first created religion. The God concept was created out of man's urgent need to protect himself from forces he could neither control nor understand. This was the elementary reason for belief in God, even as the medicine man was the forerunner of the modern scientist.

How can you protect yourself against something you cannot control? First, you must believe that though you cannot control it, there is something or someone who can. Thus, early man was compelled to conceive of a force strong enough to control all of the frightening phenomena about him. This force he called by diverse names, all more or less synonymous with "God." If this God was to control nature, He had to be stronger than nature—"supernatural," a word which is quite as primitive as the concept. It is an intellectual impossibility for man, who is limited by nature, to conceive of anything beyond nature and therefore beyond his comprehension. Since the early conception of God was limited by the outward walls of man's own being, it was inevitable that man should create an image of God very much like himself and thus part of nature rather than supernatural. We call this an anthropomorphic or human-like God, a kind of world-ruler who ruled the entire universe very much as a man rules a nation or a people. Early man created the image of a God who possessed all the elements and characteristics of a human being—a God who became angry, who loved, who punished and rewarded and reasoned. Here was a God with whom one could bargain, a God that you could cause to change His mind. In other words, man created a kind of superman whom he called God.

This, of course, accounts for the early stories in the Bible. You recall how Noah and God conversed. God became angry with man and caused the flood to come upon the earth. He became angry again when man tried to build the Tower of Babel so that he would forever be saved from the recurrence of such a flood. You recall, too, the classic bargaining story in which God lets it be known that He is going to destroy the wicked cities of Sodom and Gomorrah, and Abraham repeatedly succeeds in persuading God to change His mind. Finally God admits that if there were ten good men in Sodom and Gomorrah, He would spare the cities for their sake. Abraham, of course, had started with fifty and gradually worked his way down to ten. This was the kind of God in which the generation that wrote the story of Abraham believed.

But even this concept of God was comparatively late. Before this God appeared on the scene, there was the god of the moon, the god of the sun, the god of the earth. It was the greatness of the founders of the Jewish faith that they saw in the world not many gods who were in conflict with each other, but rather one God who was in complete control of the entire universe.

You can be very sure that when the concept of one God in the place of many gods began to make its appearance, the people who believed in many gods asked the same question that is being asked by so many today: "Are our gods dead"? There obviously were men who claimed that their gods were not dead and disavowed, disowned, and ridiculed the concept of one God in the universe.

Now, Abraham's concept of God was basically of one God, but He was the God of the Jewish people. He did not have international stature. He belonged to Abraham and to his descendants. He made direct promises to them and would be held to those promises in the generations ahead.

As the years went on, the God of the Jewish people began to take on international stature, and by the time we come to the prophet Amos, we are discussing not a God of the Jewish people but a God of all the nations of the world. Again, you can be quite sure that there were people at the time of this change who looked upon the disappearance of the localized conception of God as His death and began to bemoan what was probably the radical tendency in that day.

As man grew in intellectual stature he found it necessary to change his concepts of God in accordance with his intellectual growth. How could he eliminate the human weaknesses from his description of God without destroying the fundamental conception of a God? He found the answer by taking all of the qualities which man possessed in a limited degree and giving these qualities to God in an unlimited degree. Man was finite, so he made his God infinite. Man was limited in strength, so he made his God omnipotent or all-powerful. Man was capable of knowing only the past and sometimes the present, so he gave his God the power to see into the future as well. But all this was in vain. Despite all the attempts to change the concept of God so that He would not merely be a superman, man succeeded only in making of his God the superest man.

Thus, man was pushed almost to the extreme limits of his intellectual capacity. But not quite. When man realized what was happening, he took a new turn in his thinking. He now began to redefine the vocabulary which he used in describing his God. He admitted the weakness or fallacy of saying that God loved, hated, and so forth. He now claimed that the word "love" when applied to God did not mean the same thing as when applied to man. This was also true of other terms. To "know" something, to be "angry," to be "happy," all now had unique meanings when used in connection with God. What did they mean? No one seemed to know, because after all, God was unknowable. There were only two possible conclusions. Some maintained that human beings could not possibly understand what these words meant when applied to God. Others created new definitions which to all intents and purposes did away with the meanings of these words as used in ordinary discourse. God's "love" could mean charity, punishment, asceticism. It could include what in human terms would be regarded as cruelty.

Within our own faith the word "God" and the nature of worship have undergone many vital changes. The creation of the Temple with a priestly class privileged to offer the sacrifices to God was a new conception in Jewish life. There had been no priesthood before Aaron, the brother of Moses, was granted this privilege, but there were Jews and Jewish concepts of God before Moses. Therefore, we must assume that when the priesthood was created, placing the descendents of Aaron in a special position relative to God, there were those who shook their heads in dismay and said that the world was changing and that the God of their fathers was dead or dying.

When the Temple was in existence, sacrifices were offered as a regular part of the worship service. When the Temple was destroyed, the rabbis decreed that sacrifices were no longer necessary in order to serve God and that prayers would do just as well. You can be sure that once again there were those who believed that we were, in fact, killing the nature and person of God.

So it has gone on year after year, century after century—each era discovering, innovating, discarding, introducing new conceptions which take the place of the old.

This constant state of flux concerning the nature of God is to be found not only in Judaism but even, and to a greater extent, in the Christian faith. Here there was even more reason to challenge the various conceptions of God. Catholicism, the earliest manifestation of Christianity, realized that all conceptions of God would and could change, so it tried to create an institution which necessarily would not change except at its own speed and under its own direction, the Church. The Catholic Church, therefore, was held to have been founded by Peter at the direction of God, and it was claimed that God Himself kept watch over the workings of the Church so that it never could fall into error. The Pope is infallible not as the bishop of Rome but as the Vicar of Christ, protected from error by God Himself.

The Protestant Reformation was a revolt not merely against the authority of the Church but against this interpretation of God as given by the Church. This whole great movement within Christianity was, in a sense, a changing of man's understanding of the nature of God. It is for this reason that the Protestant reformers were referred to as heretics by the Catholics.

The point I wish to make is that almost every generation experiences an intellectual revolt against the beliefs of previous generations. The older generation attempts to fight change. The new generation attempts to bring change about by saying that the old conceptions are dead.

What is happening today and what we are witnessing, right in our own time and before our very own eyes, is one of these perennial periods of transition. The old concepts of the omnipotent, omniscient God are changing, just as the old conceptions of matter and force are being changed by virtue of the new discoveries being made almost daily in all fields of science. It is inevitable that intellectual and scientific changes should affect the beliefs of the religious institutions of the world. They are being affected but not necessarily adversely. We are looking for new conceptions, new words, and new understandings, just as we are searching for new words and meanings in every other field of human activity.

To ask whether God is dead is, in truth, merely a fad. The "Death of God" is an eye-catching phrase which excites people and brings them to synagogue or church in order to be challenged or shocked or pleased. Those who preach on the subject consider themselves heroic, whether for protecting the old or for advocating the new. The question is as silly as any question could be. If there is a God, then He is not dead. And if there is no God, then He cannot die because He never lived. "Is God Dead"? is, in actuality, a statement that the concept of God as we have known it for the past few hundred years is now in the throes of transformation. We are the generation of that transformation, and therefore we are faced with the dilemma.

Our grandchildren and their children will perhaps look back upon such discussions as this one with great amusement. How silly we were to even waste our time on such a subject. It is the same feeling that we have when we look back at some of the great religious discussions of the past, such as how many angels could dance on the head of a pin. They are meaningless to us, and what is more, they are irrelevant. Similarly, our descendants are going to look back at our present-day discussions of the "Death of God" with a feeling that we were primitive, if not childish.

We are evolving. Just where our evolving will lead is something that no one can answer. We are in the throes of an intellectual struggle to advance a conception, even as every generation before us tried to advance beyond the limitations of its own time. Sometimes the advances are almost imperceptible. Sometimes they are huge strides. I think a case could be made for the view that theological changes bear a correlation to scientific changes. In view of what is happening to our scientific conceptions, we must be ready to receive great changes in our philosophical and theological beliefs.

This does not mean that our prayerbook—which is, after all, simply a book of poetry—is meaningless. It does mean that you and I cannot accept the same theology as did the writers of the prayerbook, and that we cannot think as they thought in the field of theology, anymore than we would be willing to think as they did in the fields of science and medicine.

Let us, therefore, be joyous in the realization that man is not stagnating. We must not be fearful that there is anything morally wrong or sinful in attempting to make changes in our conception of God. Concepts do not die; they evolve and change and emerge into other concepts. Our concept of God is not dead. It is changing, and we are now in the tide of that change. Instead of condemning, fearing, or scorning those who advocate change, or strutting about in a heroic pose because we are advocates of change, let us be very grateful that we live in such an exciting and intellectually alive generation, a generation which is blessed with the opportunity to climb higher intellectual peaks and then be enabled to see further and clearer than previous generations.

The State of Israel—The Faith of Israel: What is the Relationship?

Thirty-three years ago the pious hope of the Jewish people for a homeland became a political reality. Out of the ashes and degradation of a destroyed European Jewish community, phoenix-like, there was reborn this state which had died in anguish almost two thousand years before. The emotional impact on world Jewry was intense. Although, as many saw, there were problems inherent in this event, they were dismissed or tabled in the light of the enthusiasm and thanksgiving which filled our hearts on that occasion. Now, thirty-three years after that great event in Jewish history, we are ready to consider these problems with some degree of objectivity. This can be done not because we have lost our enthusiasm or gratitude, but because the State of Israel has achieved, within these thirty-three years, a miracle of development quite as wonderful as the establishment of the state itself.

In every group within the Jewish community there are degrees of confusion as they try to determine the exact nature of the relationship which should exist between those who are of the Faith of Israel and those who live in the State of Israel.

There is a unique relationship between the land of Palestine and the Jewish faith. Palestine was the land promised to Abraham by God. ("And the Lord said unto Abram: Unto thy seed will I give this land . . . "; Genesis 12:7). Abraham is traditionally considered the founder of the Jewish faith. It is inevitable, then, that God, the man, the faith, and the land should be inextricably bound together. Through succeeding generations this relationship between the land and the faith was sustained and intensified. The historic exodus from Egypt occupies its important place in our history not only because of the freedom which was won from Egyptian slavery, but because it was the initial step in that great march across the desert toward the historic goal, the land of Palestine.

The city of Jerusalem was given eternal primacy by succeeding generations of Jews. The great religious symbol of ancient Israel, the Temple, was built on that site. But it must be understood that it was not the Temple which gave Jerusalem sanctity, but Jerusalem which gave the Temple sanctity. It followed, therefore, that a Temple could not be built on any other site, for such a Temple would not have the religious authenticity which the city of Jerusalem gave to its Temple. When, by the rivers of Babylon, the Psalmist sang his song of longing and homesickness, "If I forget thee, O Jerusalem, may my right hand lose its cunning," it was not a longing for political sovereignty or independence. It was the cry of his soul for the hallowed soil upon which he could rebuild his religious faith. No other land, no matter how rich or free, could substitute for the hills of Judea. It was only when a great pilgrimage of Jews returned from Babylon to the Holy City that the Temple was rebuilt and the faith was invigorated by the air and the earth of Palestine. The Temple was again destroyed by the Romans in 70 C.E., and only a single wall of that sanctuary remains standing.

So the years rolled by. One generation after the other uttered the phrase "Next year in Jerusalem." This hope for a return to Palestine was the most universal concept within the household of Israel. Love of Zion was felt by the pious and non-pious alike. The secularist groups in Poland and Russia sought to reach the Promised Land with the same intensity and, perhaps, even greater practicability than the religiously observant members of our faith. It should also be noted here that since the dispersion in the year 70 C.E., there never was a time when a community of Jewish people did not live in Palestine. Sometimes these communities were large and flourishing. At other times they were small and poverty-stricken. But they were there, and because of their presence in Palestine, these people considered themselves the favored sons of the Jewish faith.

Again, I must say that the love was for the land itself rather than for that which had been created on the land. Even the presence of the Temple was simply concrete evidence of the sanctity which made of Palestine a "Holy Land." Now, of course, many Jews no longer seek or pray for the reestablishment of the Temple or the sacrificial cult or the oriental pageantry of the Priests and Levites which were part of that cult. But because the land is of primary importance rather than the Temple, we can still feel a love for the land of Israel without causing any conflict between this love and the Orthodox hope for the reestablishment of the Temple in Jerusalem.

Even those who disassociate themselves completely from this love of a land based on religious tradition must see that there is a special significance and uniqueness to Israel. Is there any religious faith in the world which does not possess one spot on the face of this earth where, because of majority status, it enjoys political security and therefore can flower naturally and completely? Thirty-three years ago the answer to that question was yes; the members of the Jewish faith. Today the answer is no. Thirty-three years ago the Catholic faith had a number of lands where Catholicism was officially and unofficially the faith of the country. The Episcopal Church is the Church of England. Lutherans, Methodists, Presbyterians, Mohammedans, Buddhists, and all others possess in some degree the physical assets of a land, majority status, and political security. Only the eternal minority, the Jewish people, had been homeless and subject to the vagaries of men and time.

Now this has changed and for the first time in twenty centuries the Jewish faith has a home. The effects of this fact are not yet realized. I have known people who were brought to Israel after lives of persecution and degradation and who cannot yet believe that a knock at the door means a visit from a neighbor rather than the beginning of an odyssey to death. It takes many years to undo the havoc of an insecure life. It will also take many years for Judaism in Israel to normalize itself and realize its potential under these new circumstances. The Judaism of Israel will not be the Orthodoxy which now predominates in that country or any of the varying types of religious observance which are the hallmark of American Judaism. It will be something new, something vital, something which will be born out of security and the freedom to grow without the necessity of bending or twisting itself to meet the exigencies which are forever thrust upon the minds and bodies of a homeless people. We must be patient with the slow, tortuous steps which are being taken. The progress is slow because it is self-motivated. Judaism in Israel is not being pushed or pulled by a desire to conform.

The land of Israel has a relationship to the Jewish communities of the world in another vital fashion. It has given Jews everywhere a new dignity born of the right to choose one's place of residence and country of allegiance. Heretofore, the fear of mass emigration as an alternative to civil disability was experienced by many Jewish communities. Who would accept them? Therefore, such threats had to be met by cajolery, bribery, and the acceptance of a humiliation which almost destroyed the dignity of our people. The shame of being universally unwanted is not an easy one to bear or to explain. During the early days of the Hitler terror, the Jewish community was not shamed by Hitler's desire to rid himself of Jews. The inability of our people to live in such an atmosphere was only a source of pride. Our shame was based on the refusal of other nations to accept Jews except under conditions which were frequently humiliating and debasing.

The State of Israel has changed all of this. First, any Jew will find the gates of Israel open to him. Therefore if a Jew is a citizen of the United States, England, Brazil, or any other country in the world, it is because he chooses to be and not because he has nowhere to go. Second, the rulers of countries heretofore very cavalier in their treatment of their Jewish communities have found that the old threats are no longer met in the old way. In some instances pressure has been brought to bear to make the Jewish communities remain in a country. Although it is quite true that this latter fact does not have a direct bearing on the American Jewish community, yet indirectly it has a profound result. It is neither pleasant nor elevating to learn that our co-religionists anywhere in the world are being treated in an unseemly fashion only because of that which we share with them: our religious faith. The establishment of Israel has terminated the journey and the concept of the "Wandering Jew."

My love for Israel is not disturbed by the decadent, archaic, nationalistic lines which differentiate state from state. The problems of one nation have become the problems of another if both seek similar goals. The artificial lines between states are being erased and replaced by ideological alliances. Of course, my undivided loyalty belongs to the United States. But there is nothing in this allegiance and love of my country which diminishes, endangers, or contradicts my affection for the State of Israel. Aside from the practical benefits which Israel has given me as an American Jew, my most precious possession—my religious faith has woven into its fabric the importance of the land of Israel, without which my faith would be infinitely poorer.

There is a relationship between the land of Israel and the faith of Israel which is greater than any transient political difference or institution. Let me make crystal-clear that I do not mean that the words of Menachem Begin are Holy Writ or that the political program of the controlling party in the State of Israel is more important than the political interests of my own country. I do mean, however, that the land on which Begin stands and from which he speaks is bound up forever with my religious faith as a Jew. I want to make clear as well that I believe that when the State of Israel was born, the exile of the Jew ended.

For two thousand years our religious faith, wandering homelessly among the nations of the world, steadfastly taught the supremacy of human dignity. Now once more returned to the land of its birth, the Jewish faith will experience a new birth of life and vigor which will have a profound effect not only on Jews but on all the peoples of the world.

It was the Prophet Isaiah who said this in unexcelled elegance:

> It shall come to pass, in the end of days, that the mountain of the Lord's house shall be exalted above the hills . . . and many peoples shall go and say: Come ye and let us go up to the mountain of the Lord, to the house

of the God of Jacob; that He may teach us of His ways, and we will walk in His paths. For out of Zion shall go forth the law, and the word of the Lord from Jerusalem.

The New Anti-Semitism

Many years ago, in the magazine called *Opinion*, published by Stephen S. Wise, and edited by his son, James Waterman Wise, there appeared a fable about the king of an island whose rule was being threatened by a very shaky economy. From the daily newspapers and magazines, he learned how a man by the name of Adolf Hitler had revived the economy of Germany by blaming the Jews for all the evils that had occurred there. Not only did this help revive the economy, but in the process it helped take the minds of the people off their own bad situation. The king decided this was a very good idea, and so he called in a public relations expert and decided on the procedures of how to mount and conduct a campaign against Jews.

After he had spent a vast sum of money gaining the information he needed, preparing all the placards and signs, television shows, radio slogans, billboards, etc., he made a horrible discovery: there were no Jews in his kingdom. And so he had to go out and import Jews. He sent agents all over the world, begging, bribing Jews to come to his island. So they came, not knowing what to expect except that he had promised them great rewards for coming to his island.

When they arrived in the port, they looked out over the side of the ship and they saw all of these signs reading, "Jews Get Out," "Our Troubles Are the Jews," and so forth. They refused to disembark. And the rest of the story tells how the king begs the Jews to disembark so he could expel them. The Jews refused and the story ends with his despair.

This sounds as if it were a complete fable, and yet it is exactly what happened in Poland just a short time ago. A campaign against Jews was mounted. Now Poland is the home of anti-Semitism, or at least it was the home, and it is always easy to mount a campaign against Jews. There is only one problem in Poland today—there are practically no Jews. There are approximately ten thousand Jews, most of whom are sickly or aged, and unable to leave. When the speakers against Jews started to claim that Jews were the cause of all the labor unrest in Poland, they were just laughed off the platform. So the story in *Opinion*, which was satire, actually became a reality.

The old anti-Semitism was, of course, economic. We know that. But there was always an emotional and theological base to it. You could appeal to the ignorant that the Jews were Christ-killers and thus arouse great emotion. Pograms may have had an economic root, but they were conducted with religious fervor. In other words, whatever cynicism was behind the old anti-Semitism, it was hidden in the mud of religious bigotry which existed and could always be called upon to arouse the ignorant into action.

Hitlerism, in World War II, exposed anti-Semitism for what it really is. It was a cold-blooded attempt to take the property of citizens of Germany from them, under the pretext that they were Jewish or part-Jewish, thus enriching the anti-Semites at the expense of other people, including many whose connection with Judaism had ended generations before.

Certainly the Hitler movement had no basis in religious thought. Those churchmen who supported Hitler were looked upon not only as hypocrites but with horror by the rest of the religious world. There were men and women who stood by and even abetted the horrors and cruelties of the most inhuman activity the world had ever known. The two thousand years of Christianity were wiped out in one fell swoop. The word "Jew" had no religious connotation whatsoever. It became a racist slur, a matter of blood.

With the defeat of Hitler, anti-Semitism became unfashionable. The transitional stage between religious anti-Semitism and what now is occurring could not be bridged easily or quickly. Mankind, or Western man, had to develop new concepts. Evil has a way of manifesting itself no matter how hard we try to suppress it. Hitler taught us that anti-Semitism had no basis in religion. The average man could not call his Jewish neighbor a Christ-killer, so he had to find another reason. He found it in

Zionism. Zionism goes back long before Hitler, but it was never taken seriously because it was never a serious movement outside of the Jewish people itself. With the creation of the Jewish state in 1948, an object was created which made it possible to give voice to the old hatred. Thus today anti-Zionism has become the synonym for anti-Semitism. But neither anti-Semitism nor anti-Zionism has anything to do with religion. They are both a calculated, diabolic means of utilizing old prejudices for the specific purpose of gaining political advantage.

There is another reason why anti-Semitism and anti-Zionism are being practiced today. The wealthiest conglomerate in the world is made up of the Arab states. They have so much money that they actually do not know what to do with it. They are rabidly anti-Israel, anti-Zionist; therefore they are willing to support any movement which takes on an anti-Zionist tinge. Thus we find that most anti-Semitic groups today do not refer to themselves as anti-Semitic. After all, the Arabs are Semites. They refer to themselves as anti-Zionist. In this disguise they are able to get the drippings from the fortunes being given out to groups like the PLO, which are able to arm themselves with tanks and machine guns and light artillery and even heavy artillery, with the moneys they get from Saudi Arabia and other very wealthy Arab governments. Any small anti-Zionist group in this country today, willing to publish a tract against Zionism can secure the money and more for doing so. Is it any wonder, then, that all of the material being confiscated in Europe which is anti-Semitic and anti-Zionist in character has an imprimatur of an American organization. There is one thing about Americans, they are entrepreneurs. They have found a good thing and they are exploiting it to the hilt.

The Islamic religion is not a religion with which anti-Semites are concerned. It does not believe in Jesus, it has no overtones of Christianity at all. The Islamic faith is more rabidly anti-Christian that it ever was anti-Jewish. But religion has nothing to do with contemporary anti-Zionism. Anti-Zionism is a great business, and it is being used by everyone immoral enough to use it. It is profitable, it bothers nobody. You don't have to get into a fight. You simply print and distribute, and you will receive funds for your effort. The government of Saudi Arabia will be very happy indeed to supply you with all the money you need to continue the good work.

Yasir Arafat is quite a popular man in anti-Semitic circles. He should be. He is the fountain from which all wealth flows. The anti-Semitism which is rampant in our own country today is a cynical opportunistic activity which is able to function without expending too much effort. Anti-Semites in America do not have to risk their necks to gain whatever it is they want from their movement.

If anti-Semitism becomes unprofitable in America, it will cease to be any threat whatsoever. Of course there will always be people who will be anti-Semitic because we do not recognize Jesus. But they become even more ridiculous every day. If, as one fundamentalist preacher stated, God does not listen to a rabbi deliver an invocation, then Jesus could not have delivered the invocation, because he was Jewish. Before long people will begin to see through the religious hypocrisy and ignorance which is manifest in all this.

I could go on indicating case after case supporting my contention that the new anti-Semitism is not a religious phenomenon based on the intensity of the Christian's love for his faith. It is based on an immoral man's love for money. It is a financial exercise which is lucrative, feasible, and diabolical. It does not even have the honesty of hatred. To fight it, we must understand it. If we understand it, we will know how to deal with it. It is just a new twist of an old plot.

Is an American Dictatorship Possible?

Not too long ago, it was pointed out that there are just about a dozen or more democracies left in the entire world. For the purposes of this discussion I did not take the time to make a head count, but I know for a fact that forms of government other than democracies, dictatorships of one kind or another, far outweigh in numbers those governments in which the voice of the people is the governing voice.

Democracy demands not only a great faith in people but a faith and confidence in oneself. Dictators are born when men either lose confidence in other men or lose confidence in themselves and are therefore willing to place their destinies into the hands of others.

The Founding Fathers of this country were deeply divided in their opinions concerning the effectiveness and desirability of democracy. As a matter of fact, we in the United States do not live in what is classically termed a democracy. Our form of government is a republic. We elect those who represent us in government. We do not govern ourselves. A democracy is a government in which the people themselves make their voices heard directly in government affairs. A republic is a form of government in which people select representatives who in turn speak for them.

The Constitution of the United States is a great compromise and has always been termed such by the leading political philosophers not only of our country, but of the world. It was a compromise between those who wished a more autocratic and authoritarian form of government and those who desired a more radical kind of democracy.

In fact there are many questions which have yet to be answered in our country. When an individual is elected to represent his state or his district and casts his vote for or against a measure, what should be the measuring-rod which governs his vote? Should he use his intelligence and vote for what he himself believes is right or wrong? Or should he vote the voice of his constituency as a representative of that constituency? This problem still exists and still haunts the Congress and the Senate of the United States. Who does a representative represent, and how does he demonstrate that representation?

Democracy has certain inherent dangers. To those who would like to be dictators or who aspire to dictatorship, the people are always what is termed the "yokels." Whether they be country yokels or city yokels, they come in droves to the voting booths and can be aroused to vote one way or another if you can discover the touchstone of their selfish interests. Yokels are people who feel rather than think. They comprise blocs of voters who vote for or against a candidate because of reasons which may or may not be relevant to their own lives. I am sure that in the Irish sections of this country, anybody who came out and baldly termed the IRA a terrorist group, which it is, would be voted down.

The Social Security system of our country may be in great danger, but those who are receiving Social Security react automatically if anyone dares to discuss the possibility of altering the system in such a fashion that the benefits accruing to them may be changed.

Yokels are people who give knee-jerk reactions to words and thoughts, and can always be counted upon to behave in the same manner.

To the political philosopher, the people represent the highest tribunal, the most authoritative voice to which the government should and must pay heed. In a sense, both are right. The people are the yokels, and they are also the voice to which government must pay heed. The synthesis which is required is to create a voice of the people which will speak with intelligence and for the public interest. However, this synthesis is not easily achieved. It is a process which demands long years of education, many mistakes, misdirections, malfeasance, and constant vigilance on the part of a few who sacrifice themselves to assure the welfare of the many.

I said at the beginning that a dictatorship becomes possible when we lose confidence in others or in ourselves. Let us consider the first. It is always a very difficult thing to accept the truth that when a John Dewey or an Albert Einstein enters the voting booth on Election Day and pulls the lever for or against a given candidate, his vote counts for no more than that of a semi-literate, unemployable individual whose I.Q. falls well below 100. Both the philosopher's hand and the illiterate's hand pull the same lever, and the number which emerges is an anonymous digit with equal weight and equal significance.

Yet if we are to avoid a dictatorship, we must have confidence that between the John Deweys and the semi-literates there is a vast multitude of people who can be affected and with whom we can reason, if not immediately then in due time. If we should lose confidence in this mass of people and turn our backs on them, then the alternative is to put our government in the hands of a few chosen ones. This would destroy democracy, and eventually the few chosen would choose one. And thus we would finally wind up with a dictatorship.

Plato, despite all his brilliance, was not a believer in democracy. He believed in the rule of the few, those whom he regarded as capable of thought, reason, and logic. The would-be dictator emerges from a chosen group of people who, from their own ranks, choose one. In Russia it was the Communist Party which was the chosen group, and from the chosen group came Lenin and then Stalin.

In Germany there was the Nazi Party, the National Socialist Party. This was the chosen group, chosen to rule in opposition to the rest of the people. And from the chosen group there emerged a "chosen one"—in this case, Adolf Hitler. Thus dictatorship entails a disdain for the common man, and the refusal to deal with him as an equal, or to consider his welfare as a human being or as a participant in the political life of the country. When this occurs we encourage the emergence of a dictator.

Dictatorship is also possible when we lose confidence in ourselves. We become confused, frightened, and unsure when faced with the many crises which occur in our economic, political, and social life. Someone comes along who seems to know all the answers, or at least the answers which satisfy us. Why look further? Even if he is not altogether right, at least he offers a path which allows us to do something definite when we are beset with indecision. And so, because we are not sure of ourselves, we begin to follow someone else. Under the stress of this confusion we give up our right to disagree and then find, when failure is the result, that we cannot take back the power which was once given. This too results in dictatorship.

Therefore we must learn that no matter how confused we are as a people, no one really is less confused. Every suggestion, all directives and ideas and panaceas must be weighed in the light of our own confusion, and no man should be given credit for more intelligence or greater insight than he earns by his achievements. The man who writes a book on how to become a millionaire should not have to write the book. He should be a millionaire. Why does he have to write a book for profit if he knows the secret of how to make millions? We must also affirm the belief that no single crisis, however immediate, demands the giving up of liberty or of a right which is not only immediate and transient but is part of our heritage and our hope for the future.

Understandably and perhaps naturally, there is a tendency in many sections of our country to ignore an essential element of our democracy. Underprivileged groups, whether they be socially underprivileged, economically underprivileged, or politically underprivileged, begin to hate other groups to a degree which allows them to believe that they can achieve freedom by destroying the freedom of others. They are willing to destroy the freedom of others by putting the power to destroy that freedom into the hands of their so-called champions. From this point of view there is a possibility of dictatorship in our country.

The success of American democracy, even though its success is still to be challenged by age, since it is just a little over two hundred years old, lies in the fact that we have followed the dictates of the philosopher Rousseau, who described what he called a "social contract," namely, that each of us gives up a bit of his personal freedom in order to create a larger freedom for the entire people. We give up the right to drive at any speed we wish, to put our garbage where we desire, in order to safeguard the rights, the health of the entire commuity. That is one part of the contract.

The second part of the contract is that we give these rights to a group, but that group is always responsible to the people who gave it the rights, and the rights can be revoked whenever the people who gave them wish to take them back. This is the social contract. A people that has no confidence in others or in itself cannot create such a contract.

We are living in a very difficult age. I know this has been said ever since Adam said to Eve, as they walked out of the Garden of Eden, "Eve, we live in difficult times." Perhaps every age is difficult, but we all know there has been a change in the philosophy of government in the United States, just as there has been a change in the philosophy of government in France, and as there will be in England and in Germany.

It is a cliché to state again that eternal vigilance is the price of our freedom. Unfortunately, democracy or republicanism is something which canot be fixed or nailed down forever, and therefore possessed forever. It must be renewed daily. It must be recaptured frequently. It must be protected always.

Church and State in Israel

Since the founding of the State of Israel, the question of religious freedom has plagued both the government of Israel and many Jews who live outside of Israel. Due to political expedience, the leading Israeli political parties have always found it necessary to include representatives of the religious parties in the cabinet in order to create a working majority in the Knesset. In turn, the religious parties have utilized this strategic position to force the enactment into law of many of the religious practices which in other countries are left to the discretion of the individual Jew. The enforced observance of the Sabbath and the dietary laws in accordance with Orthodox practice has been a source of disputes and acrimonious debate both in the commercial world and in the government. Fundamental problems concerning marriage and divorce have been left in the hands of rabbinical authorities. This situation has led to grievous and frequently tragic complications. Who is permitted to be married and who is not permitted to be married are questions which strike at the most vital and sensitive areas of human life.

There is also a discriminatory attitude on the part of the rabbinical authorities in Israel concerning the establishment of non-Orthodox congregations. I use the term "non-Orthodox" rather than "Conservative" and "Reform" because both Conservative and Reform Judaism are rather flexible in their rituals and the Orthodox authorities recognize no difference between the different shades of these two branches of Judaism.

Of course, this situation is intolerable and unwarranted, and certainly it places the government of Israel in an uncomplimentary light. Reform and Conservative circles in the United States have harshly criticized the rabbinical attitude in Israel and at all of their conventions, with metronomic regularity, continue to offer resolutions of censure against the Israeli government for its discriminatory and intolerant attitude.

It is necessary to point out that the present system in Israel did not originate with the establishment of the State. Known as the Millet system, it was instituted during the period when Palestine was part of the Turkish Empire and was continued by the British, who held Palestine as a mandated territory from the end of World War I until May, 1948. Under the Millet system, each religion was permitted to create its own communal organization to administer its procedures on marriage, divorce, inheritance, and related aspects of private and family life. At the time that the Millet system was instituted, the Jewish community in Palestine was almost completely Orthodox in its religious observance, and thus, quite naturally, the communal laws it established were all in accord with the Orthodox interpretation of Judaism. When the State of Israel was founded, the Orthodox community argued that Jews should not be deprived, under a government of Jews, of the privileges which they had enjoyed under a government of non-Jews.

The Israeli secular authorities have not allowed this argument to go unchallenged. The continuous disputes create a tension and abrasiveness between religious and secular Israelis which tends to drive both further away from a common ground upon which they could live in an intelligent and cooperative fashion. The struggle continues with little sign of victory for either side, though the status quo maintains the Orthodox authorities in their privileged position.

I should like to offer an approach to a solution of this problem which I think has a degree of validity, though at the moment it probably will not be acceptable to either side.

Judaism is different from other religions in a number of ways. But perhaps one of the most significant differences lies in the fact that Judaism has attempted to spell out many concepts which in other religions are left to diverse interpretations. All religious groups, ranging from the most conservative Catholics to the most non-traditional humanists, and obviously including Judaism, use such words as "freedom," "equality," "liberty," "justice," and "rights." However, no other group explicitly spells out, for example, the meaning of "freedom" in the context of man's day-to-day living experiences. When definitions are offered they are either theological in nature or so general that they are subject to interpretations which are sometimes practically contradictory in operation. The word "freedom" may have many meanings depending on the circumstances and the environment in which it is used. Certainly, no one has a right to enjoy complete freedom, because it may well be that one person's complete freedom would, in some way, jeopardize or curtail the freedom of someone else. The question then arises, at what point does one man's freedom cease to be his right because it impinges upon the freedom of another man? Such questions must be clearly answered. When they are not, problems arise—not because of the belief in freedom, but because it becomes difficult to define freedom in practice and to apply it in a just and equitable manner.

The spelling out in detail of these generalized conceptions was the purpose of what we refer to as Rabbinic Judaism. That is why it is not the Bible that represents the heart of Judaism, but the Talmud, the principal work of Rabbinic Judaism. The Talmud must be understood as a book of common law. Though it contains extraneous matters, it is basically a set of law books dealing with the living experiences of the people who compiled it. Talmudic laws were not created de novo. They were not dictated by ecclesiastical authority and imposed upon the people without their consent. Quite to the contrary, Talmudic law frequently represents what is known today as a consensus. That is, the common practices of the people often became the law of the land. There were occasions when the rabbis, in their discussions of certain legal problems, concluded that the law should be determined in accordance with the prevalent practices of the people who would be asked to follow the law. Thus, Rabbinic Judaism is, in effect, a living, evolving law which developed from the living practices of the people for whom it was intended.

During the period when it was written, the Talmud became a legal system which represented life and practice as well as a record of the differences of opinion which existed between the groups or schools of thought involved in its writing and compilation. In the Talmud these differences of opinion are frequently described in detail, and the advocates of each side present the reasons for their point of view. An issue is brought to a conclusion in one of two ways. Either a persuasive argument finally establishes a definitive statement of policy or the question is left open for further study.

Because the Talmud is a reflection of life in a given period of our history, people in our day often consider it archaic and irrelevant. Obviously, it is. Most aspects of our life are different from those in the Talmudic period. Science, art, law, and ethics have, of course, changed both in conception and in depth due to the greater extent of our knowledge. The findings and methods of the Talmudic period are often irrelevant—not necessarily because they are in error, but because of the advances made since then in the many fields which were the subjects of discussion and debate by the teachers of that time. Sometimes the Talmudic authorities were correct in their conclusions as far as they went but did not have the knowledge to go far enough. Talmudic law is antiquated now because it was meant to suit a particular time and the particular practices of the people who lived at that time. It was not conceived by its creators as "eternal law." Therefore, the compilers of the Talmud themselves, if they could speak now, would advocate that the law must be changed in order to have relevance for the people of our time, even as they changed Jewish law in their time.

It is this view which I present as the starting point of my discussion concerning the role which the State of Israel can play that would make its existence the greatest contribution possible to the Jewish people and Judaism.

It is my belief that the separation of church and state as it exists in our own country and in some other places in the world *should not* apply to the State of Israel. Israel should seek a practical synthesis between church and state and make its national laws an extension of Jewish legal tradition. If this were done, it would revive, revitalize, and give new relevance and value to Jewish law.

I suggest, therefore, that the government of Israel should

convene a great council made up of all the leading scholars in the country. The council should consist of philosophers, scientists, rabbinical authorities, psychologists, sociologists, and others who could contribute to an understanding of the problems which beset contemporary man.

This is not as radical as it may sound. The rabbis of the Talmud were not simply authorities in religious law. Many of them were excellent astronomers. Others excelled in the field of medicine. Others were mathematicians. Still others demonstrated their greatest strength in the development of systems of logic which could be applied in interpreting old laws which resulted in the creation of a legal system suitable for use in their own time. Different rabbis were recognized for their special abilities, and when questions arose in their particular fields, though others were listened to, the specialists were usually given the last word—and the law was, in most instances, promulgated in line with their thinking. A rabbi who was a great astronomer, for instance, might have his interpretation of the law accepted if it concerned the calendar, but his opinion would not be accepted in the field of the dietary laws.

Today, scholarship is even more specialized because of the enormous body of knowledge we have acquired since the Talmudic period. Therefore, this great council should have in its membership the leading scholars in secular studies as well as religious authorities. The entire field of law should be approached not as if it were being studied for the first time but as if we were reopening the pages of the Talmud and other rabbinic literature so that the law of the land could again be a living law, to be practiced and to be meaningful in the lives of people. This living law of Israel could then be drawn upon by those who live in other lands and could be utilized to whatever extent was possible within the framework of their particular circumstances.

This was the specific purpose and function of the Talmud itself. Certainly, many laws which were applicable in the days of David and Solomon could not possibly have applied in the days of Akiva. This inadequacy was recognized by the community leaders of the time and the necessary steps were taken to adjust the laws for use in a new era. Through the use of the methods that were then acceptable, they made the necessary modifications and innovations so that these laws became meaningful in accordance with the scientific and philosophical achievements of the time. Great ingenuity was demonstrated in accomplishing this end. Even so, there were so many instances of complete innovation that the activity of these rabbis could hardly be limited to the term "interpretation."

The problem in contemporary Israel is that the Orthodox groups are trying to perpetuate a kind of Judaism which is no longer applicable to the people who live in Israel. This, in turn, has led the preponderant group of non-Orthodox Jews to seek a complete divorce from the religious law on the grounds of irrelevancy. What they mean by irrelevancy is not always apparent to Jews who live outside of Israel, because even if we wished to, we cannot possibly observe all of the Talmudic laws which might theoretically be applicable in our daily lives. The real estate laws, criminal laws, and laws of marriage and divorce that we follow are promulgated and implemented by the state in which we live, not by the rabbis, and we must abide by these laws in accordance with the rabbinic injunction which teaches: *Dina d'malchuta dina*—the secular law of the land is the law by which Jews must abide. But in Israel, the country whose very existence is part of our religious tradition, the "law of the land" is created by and for Jews. If, in the State of Israel, the pages of rabbinic literature were reopened and a new study made of all the legal aspects of individual and civil life, whether traffic laws, dietary laws, Sabbath laws, criminal laws, financial laws, or anything else, they could be reevaluated in the light of present needs and state of knowledge.

The Sabbath laws observed by Orthodox Jews are not the Sabbath laws of the Bible. They were created by later generations of rabbis and scholars who reinterpreted the Biblical law. There is no logical reason why the Sabbath laws that govern the twentieth century should not be the result of the work, study, and decision of twentieth-century scholars who reinterpret the law in accordance with the new findings available to them. The existence of a Sabbath day could be established by government edict and all official and public business could be halted. But it would be up to the government to decide which activities are essential to health and welfare and, therefore, not subject to the law. The personal Sabbath activities of the individual, whether synagogue attendance, swimming, or dancing, should be matters of choice and not compulsion. Pure food regulations and labor legislation would all be part of civil law, and those who enforce the civil law need not be rabbis, but rather men and women who, by test, have proved their competence for the task. Such a government would not be a theocracy. Anyone who, because of a personal religious commitment, desired to go beyond the civil laws would be free to do so. Thus, in the nonritualistic areas of life, civil and criminal law, all citizens, Jews and non-Jews, would be subject to the same laws.

The modern interpretation and extension of traditional Jewish law would by no means eliminate religious freedom in the State of Israel. There are many passages in Talmudic law where the religious rights of non-Jews are discussed and carefully established. In addition to the rights of non-Jews, there would have to be protection and freedom for Jews who are nonbelievers in religious ritual. This, too, is not a startling innovation. The Biblical attitude toward the "sinner" is not maintained in Talmudic law. The nature of the wrongdoer and wrongdoing underwent profound changes in Talmudic law.

The State of Israel was created out of the fabric of Jewish tradition, but it is becoming more and more alienated from the practices and spirit of true Judaism. If its laws were reinterpreted and brought up to date in the manner I am suggesting, Israel would not be simply a place of refuge for the Jewish people, or just another Levantine state in the Middle East. It would be, in reality, a living fountain from which Judaism could draw renewed strength and vitality.

Other religions have discovered that change is essential if relevancy is to be achieved. The Vatican II Ecumenical Council was an attempt by the Catholic Church to bring its religious practices into conformity with the times. This was not the first time Catholicism sought to update itself. The great Council of Trent, which lasted for almost a quarter of a century, was only one of many attempts to make Catholic dogma relevant to life.

Judaism, which is differentiated from other religions by the fact that it evolved from the actual life of the people and was not an artificially created body of law and dogma, should be the leader in such a movement. Unfortunately, we are not the leader. We are not even in the parade. The danger to Judaism is not assimilation or intermarriage. The real danger is that Judaism might become irrelevant to life. If this should occur, we would become, in truth, a fossil.

There will be strong attempts to prevent the convening of such a council from both the Orthodox groups and those who are desirous of discarding Judaism altogether. It may require many decades to create such a council, and an even longer period for its results to gain acceptance. But this should not deter the effort. Slowly but surely, the leaders of Israel must bring together their most erudite minds in all fields to discuss the changes which could and should be made so that the State of Israel can become the one state in the entire world which is governed by Jewish law.

Again, I must stress the fact that this is not an attempt to govern the lives of Jews outside of Israel. This council, its activities and its results, should be applicable only to the State of Israel, and we who live outside of Israel could utilize the portions of the law which might be followed within the environmental structure of our own lives.

The creation of such a council should be encouraged by all Jews rather than continue the dissipation of our energies only in the struggle to establish non-Orthodox groups in Israel. These groups though necessary will not solve the basic problems of contemporary Judaism or constitute a significant advance of the future fortunes of Judaism. If we face the matter squarely, almost everything which non-Orthodox Judaism has done is derivative from Orthodox practices. There are very few concepts within non-Orthodox Judaism that are either inventive or creative. Of course, this should be expected. After all, we are a very small minority group living amidst a vast non-Jewish people, and therefore our ability to be inventive and creative, though not totally impossible, is certainly very limited.

Israel represents a unique opportunity for creative activity because it is the only country in the world that is governed by Jews and where the political climate is such that the results of a conference on Jewish law could actually be implemented in life and not remain in a kind of limbo that would cause the decisions to atrophy.

It is my opinion, therefore, that the State of Israel should have as its ultimate objective a synthesizing of church and state, and that the government which functions in the State of Israel should be the result of such a synthesis, with the law of the land squarely based on the legal traditions of our people.

These developments are logically imperative if Judaism is to survive and if the State of Israel is to serve the great purpose of making that survival possible.

Will Israel Succumb to "Exile Psychology"?

Many years ago, while a student at the Jewish Institute of Religion, I had the privilege of living at the Jewish Theological Seminary. I am probably the only rabbi in America who enjoyed this dual status. My friends at the Seminary knew that I had a rather close friendship with one of the then young instructors at New York University, Dr.Sidney Hook, and they asked me whether I could have him come down and talk to the student body of the Seminary. Dr. Hook graciously consented.

I remember the content of his talk well, because it not only was true at the time but was almost prophetic. He said then that one of the reasons he would be a Zionist, if he were one, was because for the first time in history the Jews would not have to bet on the right horse, but would be in the race themselves. It was a figure of speech I never forgot.

He pointed out that we Jews always had to worry about who was in power: whether the king would be friendly or unfriendly, whether the dictator would be pro-Jewish or anti-Jewish, whether anti-Semitism would be part of the psychology of the ruling class or not. And when two factions fought, the Jewish community had to bet on the right faction. What a terrible thing it was if we bet on the wrong one and lost. Dr. Hook felt that this was not only dangerous but demeaning.

Probably no aspect of exile life so exemplified our condition as that one. Whether it was a Czar of Russia or Napoleon or Franz Josef, we were always obliged to hope that the ruler would favor the Jewish people and would tolerate our existence. This was the "exile syndrome."

In 1948 the Jewish state came into existence. It was the hope of all of us that the exile syndrome, the need to bet on the right horse, would be eliminated or diminished to an extent that would make it unimportant. And for a while this seemed to be the case. The chalutz, the pioneer struggling to clear the land, enjoying the independent life of the kibbutz, asked nothing from anyone except the right to defend himself.

The army of Israel, though not large, had a spirit which permitted it not only to defend itself but to counter-attack. They asked nothing more from the nations of the world than each was ready to give the other—namely, the mechanism and the weapons by which people defend themselves.

During the last election here in the United States, however, this disquieting symptom again emerged. Israel was no longer thinking of itself as independent but instead tried to determine which would be the right horse to bet on. In the main this psychology was thrust upon Israel by the American Jewish community. We kept trying to tell Israel which candidate was pro-Israel, which Congressman, which Senator was friendlier to Israel than the other.

To this day, what is it that fills the columns of most of the Jewish press? Will Senator Charles Percy, who is reputed to be anti-Israel, have more to say than some other Senator? Will Charles Schultz be in power and thereby bring an anti-Israel slant to the Reagan Cabinet? How will Reagan react? Will he be better than Carter? Will he be worse than Carter?

In the meantime, what is happening in Israel? An inflation rate of 150 percent is taking place. The government is split. Poverty, confusion, and complex problems are facing the nation. Israel is beginning to think in terms typical of the exile—what is better or worse for the Jews. Israel's decisions are becoming more dependent and less independent.

Whether it is a Max Fisher of Detroit telling us how good Republicans are or a Robert Strauss singing the praises of the Democratic Party, each is telling us how good his party is for the State of Israel.

Again we are standing at the door with hat in hand, exactly as we did at Versailles, and at all of the refugee conferences of the past years, when Jews could do nothing but beg, and were treated for the most part like beggars.

Ezer Weizmann came to America and flew with Carter on his campaign trail. We were not worried about the effect this had in Israel. We were worried about the effect it would have if Reagan won. The disgrace of an Israeli politician catering and kowtowing to candidates on the campaign trail in the United States was disquieting. Here in New York City I know distinguished rabbis who debated publicly, one for Carter and one for Reagan. Both of these men are ardent Zionists, and yet they were committing the cardinal sin of placing Israel once again in the role of an exile people. In great measure this unhappy development is due to Israel's dependence on the American Jewish commuity.

Prime Minister Begin came to this country just a short time ago and almost every Jewish organization demanded his presence. He must have spoken a dozen times in addition to the talks he had with American officials. He could say nothing that was new. Each time he repeated what he had said the previous time. Each time he was advised by the *shtatlanim* in the United States concerning the right course for Israel to take in the face of present conditions.

Now if it is true that the State of Israel is merely the ward of the United States, we should forget the word "independence." If it is true that the State of Israel must have the money given to it by the United Jewish Appeal, and that the United Jewish Appeal will give its money only if the State of Israel behaves in a certain fashion, then we must face the truth that though Israel flies its own flag, though Israel has its own national anthem, that flag flies only when the winds of American authority permit it to fly, and the anthem sounds only when American authority permits it to be sounded.

If the State of Israel is going to shiver and tremble, waiting for some Senator to utter his dictum on Israel, then we can no longer claim that Israel is a state unto itself. But if Israel is, as we claim it is, America's sole democratic ally in the Middle East, then Israel should act that way.

I am not an Israeli citizen and therefore I have no right to counsel that government or its people. But I do have a love for Israel, a love which causes me deep pain when I see the servility of Jewish leaders, both rabbinic and lay, as they pander to American politicians for a pleasant word or another appropriation.

I realize how urgently Israel needs the dollars which American tourists bring. But those dollars should be given freely to help Israel, not to purchase its uniqueness and self-reliance.

Americans demand creature comforts in Israel which are beyond its natural capacity. Instead of the Land of Abraham, Isaac and Jacob, it is becoming a land of Hilton, Sheraton and Holiday Inn.

Each large hotel adds not only sleeping space, but problems of labor, waste disposal, water supply, and other needs, which are sometimes overlooked in the desire for expansion.

I recall that in 1952, when I was in Israel for the first time, the gift I brought as a dinner guest was two or three eggs, and my host insisted on turning them into an omelet so that I, as the guest, could share the gift. There were few millionaires in Israel at that time. Today there are many millionaires in Israel. Today some of the magnificent homes which have been put up stand in stark contrast to the poverty which exists in the Hatikvah quarter. What promised to be a society emphasizing equality has turned into a society where, to the dismay of everyone, economic polarity exists., Israel wants Russian Jews to come to Israel and then cannot find places for them to live. The bureaucracy in Israel has discouraged aliyah. The bureaucracy of Israel has caused thousands and thousands of native Israelis to leave the country and drive taxis or open pizza stands here in the United States.

Israel has made peace with Egypt not because Carter wanted it but because it served the purpose of Sadat to have peace, and Israel took advantage of Sadat's desire. The Middle East is split, and this is the time when Israel must begin to look around, using its ingenuity to better the state of its economy and achieve greater independence for its people.

Israel must not submit to the exile psychology which you and I still possess. Therein lies the difference between an Israeli Jew and an American Jew. That is why Israel is important to us as

American Jews. That is why what Hook said in 1935 is still true today. Israel must become so strong internally that betting on the right horse is not the essential act which it now is becoming again. If Israel could drain swamps and face a hostile Arab world with the few arms it possessed in 1948, I have faith that it can maintain its dignity and independence in the present chaos of world conditions.

If the United States is going to sell Israel down the river, it will sell Israel down the river no matter how servile Weizmann or Begin or Shimon Peres becomes. If the United States wishes to have a strong ally in the Middle East, then it will depend on Israel and support Israel. But let Israel be the free and independent state which its founders envisaged and not merely a tourist attraction or a reservoir of speakers for the banquets of the American Jewish community.

Peoplehood and Demography

Reprinted from SHIV'IM—Essays and Studies in Honor of Isra Eisenstein

The "Peoplehood of Israel" has been both a belief and a goal of the Reconstructionist movement. The difficulty of achieving this goal in the Diaspora has always been evident. Varieties of national experience, pressures for accommodation to different cultural patterns, the need for political expediency, made Peoplehood a dream. But to Mordecai Kaplan, the greatest "religious statesman" of our times, it was not a fantasy. All problems were capable of solution if only there were unanimity of will. But this seemed as distant as the ultimate goal. However, even had the Jewish world achieved unanimity of will, it would have proved to be a necessary but not sufficient factor for the ultimate goal of Peoplehood. Zionism, the establishment of a Jewish state, was the essential element needed to achieve the social and cultural unity of the Jewish people. This unity would in no way diffuse or weaken the political loyalty of the Diaspora to their native countries. Judaism is a religious civilization, and would not impair political loyalty to one's country more than any other religion. Peoplehood is an element of Judaism even as evangelical activity is an element of other religions.

In 1948, for the first time in two thousand years, the establishment of the State of Israel gave the Jewish people an opportunity to weld all the components of Peoplehood and create a religious civilization strengthened by political independence. In Israel a common nationality, the absence of counter-cultural pressures, and political independence to the greatest degree possible within an interdependent political world would turn the dream of Peoplehood into a reality. To some degree this has taken place, but obstacles exist which impede rapid progress.

The problems of demography must be solved before the Peoplehood of Israel can become a viable entity. Jewish unity had previously been given its greatest impetus by the non-Jewish world. Jews were accepted, rejected, expelled, persecuted, and finally sentenced to genocide on the basis of so-called racial affinity or simply nomenclature. Only the Jews themselves recognized intrareligious differences. Cultural, religious, and philosophical conflicts were matters of importance only to the Jewish community. The Nazi machine of destruction did not differentiate between the Bundist and the Rebbe as it ploughed Jews into the ground. In many tragic instances it was only the Jews who maintained their own differences until the last tragic moment, when they realized that their common fate made internal differences completely and belatedly irrelevant.

The founders of the State of Israel were necessarily concerned with a multitude of serious problems. They had to establish an order of priorities. Sometimes, as in the case of Arab attacks, the priorities were established for them; sometimes, as with the problem of demography, the immediacy of the problem could not have been foretold. Whatever the reason, the enormity of this problem was not expected, and therefore its solution is more difficult.

The chalutzim, who constituted the bulk of the first settlers in Palestine, were, for the most part, a homogeneous group. Of course there were differences in philosophy. But these were doctrinaire differences and did not affect the basic motivation of aliyah. There was a common religion; they were either for and against the same religious tradition. There was the bond of language. Yiddish was the mother-tongue for almost everyone; Russian and Polish were also commonplace, and of course Hebrew was the most precious jewel in the linguistic diadem. The glorification of labor, the belief in the need for a reunification of Jews with the soil, and finally the belief in political and social equality as expressed in the establishment and life of the kibbutzim, created a homogeneity which made total communication possible. This did not necessarily lead to agreement, but it did mean that everyone understood the basis of disagreement.

In the years before the Holocaust, settlers came to Palestine from other parts of the world—the United States, South Africa,

Central and Western Europe. These people were absorbed quite easily into the social environment of Palestine. First, many had been born in the parts of Europe from which the majority of the early settlers came. Second, there were strong cultural bonds which again made communication easier. Shakespeare, Mozart, Pushkin, Rembrandt did not need explanation, they were merely the basis for differing value judgments. Of course a university was essential, a symphony orchestra very desirable, books as necessary as oxygen and soil. Is it any wonder that the Palestinian Jews of that time saw little if any need to create solutions for the problems of heterogeneity?

But the Holocaust produced a profound change. Jews who had never possessed a love of Zion or a desire to settle in Palestine found refuge in that land. All attempts by England, the mandatory power, to stem the tide of refugees merely made the process more difficult, but did not stop it. For the first time the original chalutzim, who had found the Balfour Declaration a convenience rather than a reason for settlement, had to deal with nonvoluntary settlers. Many of the newcomers, who came from countries overridden by the Nazis, fell under the spell of the land and became as one with the older settlers. Perhaps it would be more accurate to say almost as one, because the differences between voluntary and nonvoluntary settlers never quite disappeared. Cultural differences, too, were an obstacle. Although German and Yiddish are related enough to make communication possible, use of either language was the tool of last resort. Yiddish was considered a rival of Hebrew and therefore was looked upon unfavorably by a people striving to broaden the cultural horizons of Hebrew. To German-speaking people, Yiddish was a jargon of East European Jews, and therefore it was abrasive to their sensitivities, since German Jews had been conditioned to think of East European Jews as a lesser breed. Finally, German itself was a language with such horrible connotations that it was not included in the language departments of Israeli schools. In addition, many of the newcomers had never attained more than a reading knowledge of Hebrew, if even that, and found it most difficult to develop a fluency in Hebrew.

All these reasons, as well as others, made participation in public life extremely difficult. To make a political speech, engage in debate, or join in public forums of any kind was a practical impossibility for most of the newcomers.

Is it any wonder that these newly arrived settlers tended to remain within their own social groups, thus putting the means of integration even further out of reach? In addition, there was the problem of occupational preference. Tilling the soil and life on a kibbutz held little interest for German Jews. They had been trained for commerce and the role of middlemen. The paper-filled briefcase became almost part of their dress. Despite all these problems and differences, both groups had many characteristics in common. This was especially true in the cultural world. The Philharmonic Orchestra was enriched by excellent German instrumentalists and conductors. Artists could communicate in their own medium without concern for verb forms or vocabulary. Artisans in both groups found common ground in areas of tailoring, styling, production, each contributing his expertise. Many Germans, because of having lived in more cosmopolitan European centers, knew more than a smattering of English, a very important asset to a land with such close and frequently dependent relations with the United States and Britain. Thus, although there were many barriers between the two groups, their common ground facilitated integration and differences became less substantive. The leaders of Palestine considered "absorptive capacity" a term related to geographic rather than cultural problems.

All this underwent a profound change in 1948. The establishment of the State of Israel, one of the greatest events in the history of the Jewish people, created changes not only in the political life of the Israelis but in their social life, using the word "social" in its deepest and most extensive sense. The War of Independence created a military and political struggle between the Israeli and Arab world that has caused anguish and enmity which remain unabated to this moment. Through the open doors of Israel came the Yemenite Jews. These were people not merely of another culture but of a different historical age. They had lived servile and depressed lives in Yemen, and they came to the civilization of Israel utterly bewildered and grateful. They fit into the social framework of Israel, first, because their language was not completely alien to Hebrew, and therefore before long, language communication became possible. A second reason was the fact that under Islamic feudalism the Yemenites had been a deprived people for so many centuries that they were overcome with happiness and gratitude for their new freedom. Many were superb artisans in crafts unfamiliar to the West. In fact, most Israelis looked upon the Yemenites with the special love we give to children. They served and worked with little complaint. The Yemenites added a kind of spice to Israeli life. Their crafts, their dances, songs, and poetry, all from another age, gave Israel a special flavor making it unlike any other Jewish community in the world. Again this was evidence that the magic of the land of Israel could weld cultural differences into a new and wonderful entity.

But the Israeli-Arab enmity brought to Israel other Arabs of a different stripe. Egyptians, Syrians, Iraqis, Tunisians, Algerians, of every social and educational level, fled to the safety of Israel in the face of rising Arab persecution of Jews. Thousands came from the slums of these countries, having no means at all either to sustain themselves or to adjust to the Western standard in Israel. These were not culturally educated Germans or complacent Yemenites. Thousands and thousands of these new arrivals were merely street-wise and had lived by their wits in their countries of origin. Violence was not unknown to them. The conditions under which many had lived before made slum-dwelling in Israel familiar.

It is both dangerous and untrue to generalize about any group of people. It must be stated that many of the refugees from the Arab world were men of means, culture, and great ability. Their problems were fewer and less complex during the period of adjustment. But even as these people had little to do with the slum-dwellers before they came to Israel, they wished little to do with them now. One of the social phenomena which can be seen by Western travelers in the Islamic world is the absence of anything which might be termed a "United Islamic Appeal." Whatever the reason, Islamic people do not practice organized charity. In Iran, for example, it is difficult to convince the Jews of long Iranian background rather than European origin to contribute to organized charity. As Islamic people they seem to believe that each should take care of his own immediate family, and philanthropy should be limited to "baksheesh," small handouts.

Thus in Israel the care of disadvantaged refugees from Arab countries was left almost entirely in the hands of the government. I think it would be true to say that the numbers of people and problems created by this exodus from the Arab world were overwhelming.

The land failed to work its magic. The government had to face mores dealing with family life, marriage, religion, never before experienced. In addition these were people who were quite familiar with affluence and political pressure even if they lacked these assets themselves. The Israeli government hoped that service in the armed forces would help the adjustment process for some, and undoubtedly it did. Many could not serve in the armed forces, and those who did returned to the same environment which they had left. There was one difference. A large number had been good soldiers, loyal, brave, but also observant. They realized that there were few of their group serving as officers. The fact that they were not prepared for this role was of little importance, for it was also true that very few could hope to reach the educational level which would make them eligible for these posts. This created a degree of dissatisfaction and resentment which has taken many forms. Crime, poverty, and social deprivation are interwoven wherever they exist. Israel is no exception. The crime rate there has risen, the nature of crime has become more violent, political demagoguery has manifested itself. "Protectzia," formerly limited to social and political areas of life, has been altered to include the protection racket so familiar in our own country.

The problems have not yet reached the proportions which exist in the United States, but if the trend is to be stopped, it must be done quickly. Social struggle is not endemic to one group. If one deprived group seems to ease the situation by anti-social activity, other groups will decide to utilize the same tactics. Adding to the difficulty are those people who believe that anti-social behavior is excusable if caused by poverty. This has proved to be a tragic even if well-meaning error.

Happily the State of Israel is confronting the situation, and despite the multitude of demands on its economy, has started to eradicate the causes. Schools, not prisons, are being created for delinquent children. Disadvantages must be removed not by rhetoric but by actions which remove the root causes of the problem. Israel feels obligated to expand this program not only as a humanitarian act but in order to fulfill the hope of Jewish Peoplehood. In the lexicon of Reconstructionism, this is a religious obligation as well as a social consideration.

The latest demographic problem facing Israel is the arrival of Russian Jews. If this great group of Jews had arrived twenty-eight years ago, there would have been fewer problems. The number of Russian-speaking Jews in Israel would have made communication easier. The system of the kibbutz and the general emphasis on social equality so prevalent during the earliest days of the state would have found echoes in the hearts of Russian Jews. The only reason for mentioning this fact is not to dwell on a past which cannot be relived, but rather to find some small hint which will enable the state to solve the problem of adjustment which is trying the hearts of us all.

Soviet Jewry is not finding its home in Israel to the extent we hoped for. Thousands are going to the United States, Canada, Australia, and other countries. Many who go to Israel find the difficulties so great that they leave. Certainly we all recognize that the problems faced by Israel are so overwhelming that adding to its burden seems to be unreasonable. But the ache for Peoplehood persists. The challenge cannot go unmet or the situation untreated. For example, why do we feel that Soviet Jews who opt for countries other than Israel should be prepared at schools in Rome for the linguistic and social difficulties they will face? Perhaps those who are Israel-bound should be equally or even better prepared. Soviet Jews have been culturally bombarded throughout their lives with anti-Western and anti-religious propaganda. They come from a country which is militarily secure, culturally advanced in many areas, and, for the most part, economically stable. Despite these advantages, thousands of Soviet Jews are willing to sacrifice everything for freedom and Peoplehood, which persist in spite of the Soviets' attempt to destroy them. Should these people be sent directly to Israel, where hearts are full but larders empty, or should they too be given a longer period of training, acquainting them with the language, history, and problems of Israel? There would be little difference between the cost for such a program and the need to support them in Israel. Even if the cost in dollars was great, the profit in terms of spiritual adjustment would be even greater. This longer period of training might ease the culture shock brought on by the change in climate, language, social values, and economic problems.

We, who believe in the Peoplehood of Israel, look to the small State of Israel as the fulcrum on which the Jewish world can elevate itself. For two thousand years we have awaited this opportunity. We cannot allow it to slip through our fingers. We must recognize that Israel is not the homogeneous land which was our age-long dream. History has decreed that it become a heterogeneous land, beset by all the problems implicit in such development.

My appeal for understanding this fact is not directed to the leaders and people of Israel; they are already aware of the situation. The appeal must be made to the Jewish people outside the land, who must realize that Israel is not simply a place of horas and happy farmers always ready to burst into song. Israel is now a land beset by demographic differences which cannot be brushed aside or ignored. In the face of all difficulties, Peoplehood remains the ever-present and ever-nearer goal. To paraphrase the *Ethics of Our Fathers*, it is not for us to reach the goal, but neither are we free to turn from the road which will reach it.

A Black Market in Coffins: Did Hitler Really Win?

The recent earthquake in Southern Italy which claimed over three thousand lives was a terrible catastrophe, but it was not an immoral act. It was an act of nature which, under present circumstances, could not have been prevented or even foretold. What followed, however, was a catastrophe of even greater proportions, and it was immoral to a degree which was unbelievable. We have learned from many sources that following the catastrophe there arose a black market in the sale of coffins. Families were being held up by excessive costs for the terrible duty of burying their dead. The callousness which this indicates is almost inhuman.

In addition to the black market in coffins, which was partially offset by the funeral directors in America, who sent a thousand coffins to Italy, was the black market in the relief material sent to that stricken country from all over the world. The food, clothing, tents, and medical supplies were stolen and held for those who could pay the highest prices. I don't know how you felt about this matter, but to me it was a chilling experience which indicated that man's inhumanity to man has sunk to a new low.

Forget for a moment that this was taking place in a country just hours away from Rome, the center of the Roman Catholic Church, that all this was being done with the complete knowledge of the Church and that the Church did little if anything to stop the gouging of the living who were trying to pay their respects to the dead. There was very little said from the Vatican window about the horrors being perpetrated. No one was excommunicated. No one was denounced. The Church was strangely silent. I am quite sure that it was not because the Church approved of what was going on, but because the Church is involved in matters which are not immediately germane to the lives of its people.

The Roman Catholic Church has vast powers in Italy, both legally and morally, and yet those powers were not utilized. Perhaps I am being unfair. Perhaps they were applied. But the newspapers in this country carried no news of such application. I therefore must assume that because a word from the Holy See would have had tremendous importance in this situation, lack of news concerning such a word means that it was not spoken. However, I am not dealing with the cruelty, the inhumanity, and the callousness which Italians showed for each other in a time of great need, but with another aspect of the story which I think is equally important.

I can recall similar catastrophic events which took place before 1939. Somehow at that time there was a greater valuation placed on human life, especially within the borders of a single country. An earthquake demanded the immediate attention not only of the government of the country in which it occurred but of all good people throughout the world. Help was rushed because life was dear and precious. Something has happened to the world, something which has changed the point of view of so many people. I believe that World War II and the rise of Hitler and the creation of what is known as genocide gave the world a new sense of values which accounts for what is happening today. Everyone believed that six million Jews were killed and it was a problem for the Jewish people. First, it was more than six million Jews. Over thirteen million people were killed by the Nazis, among them six million Jews. And the killing of Jews results in a psychology which is always a corollary to the killing of anything or anyone.

It is an interesting fact that in the Jewish faith, a man who acts as a *shochet* must pronounce a blessing each time that he slaughters a chicken. And the blessing is a prayer that those who utilize the flesh of the chicken will prove worthy of its sacrifice. The rabbis, in commenting on this, said that when one kills as a profession, whether it be men or chickens, a callousness results which is dangerous and which can cause great immorality among the killers. This has, unfortunately, proved to be too true.

Germany created a death machine which was impersonal, without mercy, without pity. It gave to one group of men the right to torture and destroy other men and women. It made heroes of those who destroyed, not in warfare, but in a cold-blooded fashion. It created a degree of cruelty in the lives of those who committed these acts which had never before been the lot of so many human beings under similar circumstances. When the Germans came to Italy, Italians turned the Jews over to the Nazi war machine for deportation and ultimate death. They knew they were doing this. They knew what the result of such actions would be. This did not stop them. You cannot say that this is a normal, usual occurrence. After all, Denmark too was an occupied country, and yet the Danes did not turn over their Jewish population. On the contrary, they fought with every bit of strength they possessed, every stratagem they could devise, to save the Jews. To them human life was valuable and dear, and it remains dear to this day. But the great bulk of the population of Europe was tainted and spoiled by the poison of Hitlerism. And the greatest and most dangerous element of that poison was the refusal to recognize the value of humanity. Human beings were no longer important as such. Human beings were crowded into cattle cars in a fashion which would not have been tolerated in the case of cattle. Many died en route. The stories of what took place not only in the death camps but on the way to the death camps are heartbreaking.

When people are told to despoil corpses of teeth and hair, they may become sick for the first day or two, but after a while they become hardened and the task becomes just that, another task to be fulfilled, like chopping wood or butchering a calf.

During the occupation by Hitler, Italian turned against Italian. It does not matter that some were Jewish and some were not. They had been neighbors, sometimes for generations. They spoke the same language, enjoyed the same music, ate the same foods, and yet, in the face of Nazis they became strangers to one another; not only strangers, but enemies. You cannot do this to a people and think that they will remain uncontaminated when the catastrophe passes. Hitler was a moral catastrophe who destroyed millions of people. The earthquake was a catastrophe which killed thousands of people. But the reactions of those who stayed alive had been conditioned by the years of Hitler and resulted in the callous and unbelieving degeneracy to which human life fell during the tragic earthquake.

Hitler's aim was not merely to establish political power over Europe, he also wished to establish a set of values in which he believed, and in which those around him believed. The question we must ask ourselves, based on what happened in Italy and what has happened in other parts of the world, is: did Hitler lose the war or did he really win? He may have blown himself up in a bunker, he may have destroyed his body, but I am afraid that his value system could not be destroyed by dynamite or gunpowder.

There are Germans, living in South America today, who are known to be mass murderers. They live in splendor as honored guests of the state. They cannot be touched, they cannot be punished. Even in Germany and Austria it is becoming more and more difficult to convict those who participated in acts of genocide. It is not becoming more difficult because there is a lack of witnesses. It is becoming more difficult because the whole attitude of humanity is changing. In the city of Atlanta, fourteen black children are abducted and murdered. It is featured in newspapers, but not with the headlines one would imagine. The Klan has a firing range where it is teaching young people how to be terrorists in our own country. We are not shocked, we simply say it should not be done. But there is no rising up, no denouncing of the acts of these terrorists by both Jews and Christians. The only thing which prevents the Ku Klux Klan from marching in a parade is the lack of a permit.

I am not pointing a finger at Italy, I am pointing a finger at ourselves. I am pointing a finger at France and at England, where not only acts of anti-Semitism but acts of violence are occurring with greater and greater frequency. Do you think that before 1939 Arab terrorists would have been welcomed in the countries of Europe? They might not have been captured or punished with the degree of severity that we would have liked, but certainly these terrorists would not have been given offices, territorial rights, and voices in the council of nations. Hitler taught us that murder can be accepted, that terrorism is not a horrible thing. Germany today is a respected nation of the world, though so many are still alive who were part of that terror.

Thus I look with great sorrow on the tragedy in Italy, not only because of the death of so many people but because of the horrible callousness which marked the behavior of those who were fortunate enough to remain alive. A black market in coffins is an indication that Hitler really did not lose the war. We still have that war to win. It will not be easy, it may even take generations to erase from the human psyche the acceptance of murder, torture, and terror which now exists in every corner of the world. South America, France, England, India, Afghanistan, any place that one can mention, including our own United States, has to be cleansed of this great and terrible victory which Hitler achieved even in his defeat.

The United Nations Is Thirty-six Years Old . . . Old . . . Old

Thirty-six years ago, the nations of the world gathered in San Francisco to establish what was to be called the United Nations. A charter was written—a covenant designed to prevent a recurrence of the holocaust through which the world had passed since 1939. Historical events do not last long in the minds of men. Somehow, the pressure of the present pushes history into the back streets of our mentality.

Therefore, it is not redundant on my part to remind you of the tragic era through which the world had passed in the "sick years" from 1939 through 1945. I do not refer only to the six million Jews who were killed by the Nazis. In addition to these six million, there were more millions in Russia who were killed by the Nazis, and if one were to count the number of deaths throughout Central Europe and Eastern Europe, I think we could say that the Nazi war machine was responsible for the death of at least twenty-five million people.

The six million Jews occupy a special place in this spectrum of horror because they were killed not as soldiers who were fighting against an enemy, not as inhabitants of lands through which an enemy had to pass, and not as occupants of cities such as Leningrad which the Nazis wished to capture. These were people who were killed simply because they bore the name Jew. They were thrust into ovens, buried in nameless graves—the geniuses, the artists, the physicians, the painters, as well as the ordinary men and women, who loved each other and were loved by many. Although the six million are a special horror, they do not diminish the horror of the others who were also victims of the Nazi war machine.

However, this was not the only area of the international conflict. We must also think of the millions who were slaughtered by the Japanese in their conquest of the Far Eastern world, in their march from their homeland to the very gates of Australia. We must remember those who were killed by the Allies in the attempt to stop both of these war machines—the millions of Germans and Japanese and others who were the victims of war and slaughter.

The men and women who gathered thirty-six years ago in San Francisco had been witnesses to the slaughter of some seventy-five to one hundred million people. The war-weariness, the utter despair which gripped them, made the hope of a United Nations Organization something more like the dream of a Messianic age than a political document and organism. But it was not long before the countries which had suffered so bitterly began to plant the same seeds which had resulted in the harvest of horror before.

The world began to polarize around the two great nations, the United States and the Soviet Union. In the United Nations itself, the whole process began to flounder. In 1948, the United Nations partitioned Palestine and created the State of Israel. This was the act of a youthful organization. Young people are prone to be more adventuresome. They attempt new tasks without fearing that their past failures will again result in failure. They are willing to learn, even if they are hard-headed and impetuous in the process. Above all else, young people have a degree of hope, and this is essential if youth is to have the potential and the glory which belongs to it by right.

What was given to the newly formed State of Israel was a very small area. Nevertheless, because it was the work of the United Nations, because it was at last a recognition of the rights of the Jewish people, it was accepted and the State of Israel was born. The Jews would have been more than happy to accept whatever limitations had been placed upon them geographically, though those limitations were onerous indeed!

This act of the United Nations was something wonderful. If it had worked, I dare say, the United Nations would have been encouraged in its attempts to clarify and perhaps to solve many of the other problems which confronted the world. But the ink used to sign the document was not yet dry when the Arab world decided that this was an injustice to them that had to be rectified through warfare. And so, in 1948, on the very day of the Independence of Israel, war was declared for the purpose of undoing that which the United Nations had accomplished.

The English troops in Palestine left the Jews in a state of defenselessness and turned their major arsenals over to Arab terrorists. Those of us who lived through that period remember it well, and we are not quick to forgive the callousness of a British military command which had itself passed through a terrible ordeal and was now almost guaranteeing the death of a state for whose creation England itself had voted. History did not work out according to the plans of the English, who had hoped that the young state would find itself in such a precarious position that it would reinvite English intervention.

So in 1948 there began a power struggle. The State of Israel and its Arab neighbors were the pawns in this fight, which has continued with unabated vigor and terror up to the present time. This was the beginning of similar confrontations all over the world. It is my contention that had the United Nations stood by its decision vis-à-vis Israel, and had the Arab nations been forced to accept what the United Nations had decided was just and right, there would have been less chance of a Korea, of a Vietnam, of a Hungary, of a Czechoslovakia, and of a multitude of other minor skirmishes which have marred the history of our family of nations.

What has happened now to the United Nations is that its continuous failures in international politics have obscured its successes. The United Nations has served many wonderful purposes. In the areas of health and trade the United Nations has succeeded. But these pale into insignificance when we are faced with the real horror of war.

The United Nations, having utilized so much of its energies in attempting to solve the problems created by its own weaknesses and mistakes, has grown old in service. We know the signs of old age. We know that the old people tend to be garrulous, especially about the past. They are quite willing to send others to do battle while they limit their activity to a verbal conflict. We know that there is an inflexibility as we grow older, based on habit and the fear of changes with which we cannot cope. Therefore, we tend to say that what is, is best, and that what might be is not desirable. We carry on old feuds.

The United States and the Soviet Union, within the framework of the United Nations, continue with the feud that has marked the life of the world organization since almost the beginning of its existence.

Is there anyone who believes that the United Nations as it stands today is going to be the means of securing world peace? Or is it rather a forum in which people talk, not to each other, but at each other and to their constituencies at home. The United Nations has become calcified, inflexible, garrulous, and argumentative. It refuses to face new challenges, to take on new responsibilities. It is unfortunate that many nations are not sending their top talent to represent them. Instead they send secondary talent. This is especially true of the major powers. Of course, when the crises arise they send their first teams to take the field against the first teams of the other nations. However, the day-by-day activities, which should be in the hands of experts, are not! This is not a universal practice, but too often it is the practice of the United States, Great Britain, the Soviet Union, and France. These represent the power establishment within the United Nations.

Finally, the independence of thought which was part of the United Nations' dream has disappeared. I think that if the Soviet Union announced that the moon is made of cream cheese, there would be at least thirty-six votes in the United Nations confirming this statement. The United Nations was and still remains the world's greatest single hope for peace. But the United Nations as it is now constituted is an old, old man, and it must give way to some reorganization which will allow greater independence of thought on the part of its constituent membership. I do not say that this is possible, but what the ingenuity of man created and destroyed, it can possibly rebuild.

I hope that it will not take a third great conflagration to cause the nations of the world to recognize the necessity for reorganizing and revitalizing the United Nations.

The Thirty-Million-Dollar "Gate"

A short time ago, a prizefight was held at Madison Square Garden. The price of tickets for the spectators and those who watched via television throughout the country and overseas brought the amount of money earned by this fight to somewhere between thirty and forty million dollars. This is a rather huge sum, and represents, perhaps, the record amount of money taken in by such an event in the history of the sport.

No one complained about the amount of money that was raised in this fashion. Each fighter received, for his forty-five minutes in the ring plus fourteen minutes of rest between rounds, making a total of fifty-nine minutes of labor—less than an hour—two and one-half million dollars. There were no cries of outrage or great editorials flooding the newspapers or the television world, questioning the use of such vast sums. In fact, quite to the contrary, outside Madison Square Garden there were people who were willing to pay even greater amounts to buy seats from those who had already paid exorbitant amounts. There was no arm-twisting, there were no speeches in opposition, no strikes, no work actions. These millions of dollars were raised easily and with almost everyone's approval.

There was just one very peculiar coincidence which occurred during the very week in which the fight took place. The mayor of the city of New York announced that due to a deficit of between thirty and forty million dollars, almost the exact sum of money which was raised by this prizefight, there would have to be a cutback in the city's educational system. This cutback would consist of the firing of almost ten thousand teachers, the elimination of special afterschool programs, the elimination of adult education programs and a series of other educational activities—all of which would have seriously affected New York's intellectual life.

On the one hand, we had forty million dollars being paid to

witness two men batter each other, and on the other hand, the lack of that exact sum of money resulting in the serious curtailment of the educational system of a great city. I wonder what would have happened had the people who paid one hundred, two hundred, and three hundred dollars for a seat at that fight, or ten dollars to watch the fight over closed-circuit television, been approached and asked to contribute the same sum of money to the educational needs of our city, or our country, and thus do away with the educational deficit. I wonder whether there would have been as spontaneous a spirit of giving as there was for the fight. I say I wonder, but that is merely rhetorical. I know that there would have been an outcry of outrage against the confiscation of people's wealth for the terrible purpose of maintaining educational standards.

I do not wish to be misunderstood. I have no complaint against the fighters who received their money. After all, if people are blessed with the kind of intelligence which permits them to spend almost forty million dollars to witness such an event, why shouldn't they take advantage of it? What does frighten me, of course, is the fact that events such as this fight, and the amounts of money being paid to contemporary gladiators, are so reminiscent of the last days of a disappearing Roman Empire.

We are living in an age when the value system which governs our lives, our government, and our recreation has degenerated into the satisfaction of all sensual appetites. It is not enough to repeat the same event in order to achieve the same results. Throwing Christians to the lions became a bore after a while. The Christians didn't have a chance. Only those who were sadistic found any pleasure in watching hungry lions tear human beings apart. They had to change the act, and so they brought human gladiators in. At first the gladiators used swords, but that became tiresome, and so they began to create new types of weapons, one more horrible than the other, which brought the fight to a faster conclusion, and caused the victors to be almost as bloody as the losers. Each time, a new trick had to be invented which would involve the interest of the spectators. Circuses always require greater and greater risks on the part of the performers in order to win an audience.

I am rather certain that if the two men who made this thirty million dollars possible should fight again, it would not be quite as easy to raise that amount of money. We have already seen these two fighters, and there would have to be an added attraction of some kind in order to make the same people spend the same amount of money.

The trouble with education is that we cannot change the act. Education is a process of teaching people the same material that we ourselves were taught. It is the undramatic, unromantic process of giving people a knowledge of reading, writing, and reasoning. To a crowd that is willing to pay forty million dollars to watch two men beat each other, the goal of reasoning, by definition, seems most unattractive and frankly undesirable.

What is happening in this one area of life is happening in many other places as well. We used to be satisfied to watch a rodeo during which men tried to ride horses that were unbroken or to rope calves or to ride with great artistry. We all know that this has palled. Now, the horses are strapped in such a fashion that they are in intense pain and buck in order to get rid of the rider—this is to make it more exciting.

If riding horses loses its attraction, we then turn to automobile racing. But automobile racing in a special racing car has only a certain amount of attraction. It is a lot more fun to have stock car races, where we bang into each other, we destroy each other's cars, and the last one able to move is declared the winner. What this proves is anybody's guess. The fact that people are willing to pay their hard-earned money to witness this kind of event does prove something about the intelligence and the sensitivity of our population. But this is a growing tendency in American life. We are asking to see more and more dangerous events, and we are paying higher and higher admissions to see the kinds of events which arouse, titillate, thrill, and provide everything but education.

Many colleges are on the verge of closing. A forty-million-dollar grant to any college in the country would give it a new life. A gift of two and one-half million dollars to any department of a college would provide that college with a number of professors for a lifetime. They will not be given two and one-half million dollars. But fifty-nine minutes of beating another man to a pulp will be rewarded with two and one-half million dollars. Such is the state of the country in which we now live.

The thirty- or forty-million-dollar gate which was the result of matching two men in a prizefight reflects the intellectual, emotional, and spiritual state in which our country now finds itself. It is a state of mind which will permit us to spend billions of dollars on armaments, an expenditure which in the last analysis is meaningless, because we already have enough armaments to destroy the entire world. Just whom we are going to destroy after we destroy everybody on earth is a little difficult to imagine. Yet we continue to do it.

There are some questions asked, there are doubts raised, but when the votes are counted, we are ready to spend the money to create the weapons and machinery of killing. We are not ready, we are not willing, and we are not capable of spending a small percentage of that money in order to give the people of this country a better education, a better way of life, a better reason for life.

How will it all end? I don't know. The road down which we are traveling is a very dangerous one. It has a momentum and almost a life of its own. Whether we are able to turn this road in another direction, whether we are able to begin to see what values are really worth struggling for, worth paying for, I am not at all sure, and I do not think there is anybody in this country who can predict the results with any degree of accuracy.

I do know that such a series of events, such a program of action, will usually result in a catastrophe, and then we may be awakened to the need for change. I can only hope—and I say this with the full realization that I am being a kind of Jeremiah, never a popular role to fill—that the catastrophe which will inevitably occur, and which will serve the purpose of making us want to change the road on which we are now traveling, will not be so great and so final that it will make change impossible.

Perhaps the only recourse we can have at such a time is the prophetic faith which allowed our teachers in the past to view catastrophe with a feeling that we were not put here on earth, and permitted to survive for so many years, for the sole purpose of self-destruction. Let us hope that this is true; it is with this faith that you and I will find it possible to face the future.

Maybe We Need "Truth in Living" Too!

A recent trend in consumer protection is the legislation designed to establish what is called "truth in lending." It is the purpose of these laws to make clear to borrowers exactly the amount of interest they will be paying on their loans, or on the money which they owe for merchandise purchased on credit. This was a long-awaited and necessary reform. It does not, of course, prevent people from undertaking obligations which they cannot meet; it merely tries to make clear what those obligations are. The intelligence of the borrower is the guide to the amount of the borrowing and the purpose for which the borrowing takes place.

When I read the words "truth in lending," I could not help but think that there should be a kind of "truth in living" as well. Truth in living, like truth in lending, will not add intelligence or wisdom to people. It will simply clarify the obligations, the responsibilities, and the duties with which we are faced. This is especially true in our day. Our society is fast becoming even more polarized than it was in the past. Those who wish to keep things as they are, are willing to paint the situation rosier than it is. This is done not by lies, but by allowing for misinterpretation of the facts as they are presented.

One of the great creative literary accomplishments of our time was the euphemisms with which the military complex was able to devise in order to cover the blunt fact that the war in Southeast Asia was really not diminishing at all, but escalating. What a wonderful thing it would have been if, instead of those euphemisms, we had been told the truth. Then, at least, we could have made up our minds as to the wisdom of what we believed, or the wisdom of those who asked us to follow a particular road of action.

But truth in living is not simply a demand which should be made on those who wish to keep things as they are. It is equally important that those who wish to change things be truthful in stating what it is they want to change, and how they want the change accomplished.

The tactics of Madison Avenue, which attempt to dress up unpleasant truths in a pleasant garb, are not limited to any one sector of our society. Politics is not a calling limited to members of the establishment. There are politics in labor unions as there are in corporations. There are politics in the radical movements as there are politics in the conservative movements. And politicians are for the most part of one kind. They attempt to achieve success by interpreting their actions, their aspirations, their programs in the best light possible. They will choose whatever statistics serve their purposes, and they will omit those figures which do not serve their purposes. They will seek an interpretation of trends which enhances their reputations, and they will avoid the use of any information which tends to prove them incorrect.

This, of course, has been going on for many, many generations. The problem which exists today, making the situation more serious than it was before, is that lines of communication are now more easily accessible and far more effective. This, in a sense, is a paradox. It would ordinarily be thought that if communications are easily achieved and mass media are available, the ability to hide the truth would be more difficult, the techniques of evasion would be more discernible. On the contrary, the ability to communicate to the masses has given those who control the means of communication the ability to mislead, to misrepresent, to misquote, to misinform. Freedom of the press, which is now almost total, has given those who possess that freedom a means of saying whatever they want, and we are not prepared to evaluate these statements in an adequate fashion. The American people has been accustomed for so long to trust the printed and spoken word that we have not yet learned that deceit and subterfuge are as much a part of our lives in the arena of public affairs as they were in the area of lending and credit.

There is another aspect to this question which is not quite as obvious. One of the reasons for the truth in lending bill was the fact that the truth was actually told about the moneys that were owed, but it was told in such a fashion that it was incomprehensible to those who did the borrowing. To talk about *X* percent per month but to omit the total cost per year was not to lie, but to tell the truth in a fashion which was actually not truthful.

In public life we do this through the double-talk of statistical tables. It is always reminiscent of the brothers, one of whom earned fifty thousand dollars a year and the other earned two thousand dollars a year. Therefore, between them they averaged twenty-six thousand dollars a year. That is the truth. But the brother who earned two thousand dollars a year was starving to death, while the brother who earned fifty thousand dollars a year was living well. They didn't live on the average, they lived on the actual. Thus, when we talk today of what the average national income is, we forget those who are high up the economic ladder raise the average, and those who have little or nothing are told that they live in an affluent society because the average income is so much higher than it was five or ten years ago.

But public life is not the only area in which there should be "truth in living." There is also the area of academic life. There is no royal road to learning, and it is very easy to state that something which you are learning is irrelevant. Shakespeare is irrelevant. Milton is irrelevant. Beethoven is irrelevant. You can't earn a living with it.

The truth is that more and more people are finding it difficult to discipline themselves to learning, and therefore they use the excuse that the materials are irrelevant. It is an interesting phenomenon that even in the area of Black studies the same conditions often exist. There is certainly a need for the world to have a better understanding of the contribution of the African peoples to the culture of the world. There is a need for the American people to understand the contribution which Black people have made to the life and culture of our own country. But this is not a matter of emotionalizing, it is a matter of intellectualizing. It is a matter of study, of research, of demonstrating a grasp of the material, and the ability to prove the possession of it.

The moment this happens on a college campus where Black studies have been instituted, and those who take the courses are required to demonstrate a mastery of the material, those who were fighting for the institution of Black studies begin to declare that it is irrelevant or they damn it with the charge that it is resembling white studies to a great degree and therefore should be changed.

Family life is suffering from a lack of truth in living. Parents and children talk about each other rather than to each other. Parents bemoan the attitudes and life-styles of their children. The children ridicule and despise the life-styles of their parents. I guess it must be said that there is a little truth on each of the sides and a great deal of falsehood and misrepresentation on both. A great deal of the resentment which exists in family life is due to the fact that both parent and child find it difficult to bear their respective responsibilities.

Parents find it difficult to give of themselves and therefore give of their means as a substitute for the more difficult task. They resent children who do not appreciate the substitution. Children who call their parents hypocrites because they recognize the difference between the words and acts of their parents commit the same kind of hypocrisy, covering their own lack of responsibility with euphemisms such as "new life-style." They "give up" on the establishment rather than attempt to change it. And when and if they try to change it, they do so in a manner which they know in advance is doomed to failure. But the failure is laid at everyone's door but their own.

Finally, there is the truth in living which we must practice when we deal not with others but with ourselves. Sometimes we can afford to fool others. Sometimes it may even be necessary to do so. But it is never necessary and it is never wise to fool oneself. It is also the most dangerous kind of falsehood. To be honest with oneself is to possess an anchor. To give up that honesty means simply to be afloat without direction, without control.

To achieve truth in living is much more difficult than to achieve truth in lending. After all, no one forces you to borrow money. However, unless you are mentally ill and wish to commit suicide, you are forced to live, and therefore you are faced constantly with the need of achieving truth or falsity in your life. There are no other options than these.

Just as self-appraisal is the most important kind of honesty to possess, it is also the most vital kind of honesty to achieve. Honesty with oneself involves ego. When others attack our ego, we can hide behind the shield of self-confidence. When we attack our own egos, self-confidence is lost, and we stand naked before the winds of reality.

But the strong person is not one who thinks he is strong by virtue of self-deception, but one who knows he is strong by virtue of integrity and honesty. Unfortunately, we cannot pass legislation to ensure truth in living, that is a voluntary act. This makes achieving truth in living far more serious. But once achieved it becomes far more valuable.

The Czars Are Laughing

If we were to search for a country which could be labeled "the classical home of anti-Semitism," we would not be wrong in naming Russia as that country. Before World War I, the Jewish population of Russia, numbering from five to six million, was kept apart from the rest of the country socially and legally.

The Czars of Russia were easily persuaded that the simple Russian peasants had to be protected from the clever Jews, and using this reasoning as an excuse, they consistently refused to emancipate the Jews. Even Alexander II, who was the most enlightened of the Russian Czars and whose reign is looked back upon by the Jews of Russia as the "Golden Age," never went further than trying to give Jews a better chance to work toward assimilation.

One of the great literary lights of Czarist Russia, Dostoyevsky, openly voiced in his letters anti-Semitic views which were so sharp that the Soviet editors of his correspondence were embarrassed and censored them. Even Turgenev, one of the most enlightened of Russian nineteenth-century writers, had no inhibitions against expressing anti-Semitic views in private. However, both of these men preceded the emergence of official Russian anti-Semitism, which shocked the civilized world. The pogroms of 1881, the Beilis case, and the issuance of the *Protocols of the Elders of Zion* were all part of the terror which permeated Czarist Russia. The results of this policy were momentous.

Between 1870 and 1914, the vast Jewish emigration from Russia—including Poland, which then formed an integral part of Russia—virtually created, or at least enlarged beyond recognition, the Jewish communities of Britain and the United States. Another result was the birth of Zionism, the dream of founding a Jewish state in Palestine. Another direct result of official policy toward Russian Jews in the nineteenth century was that many of them threw themselves into revolutionary activities.

However, many of the revolutionists did not join the movement to emancipate Jews, but rather to emancipate the international working class. It was their hope that when a Communist revolution achieved its success, anti-Semitism would disappear along with all of the other persecutions taking place in the world. It was their hope that with the creation of a great Communist International, religion itself would cease to be a necessity, and therefore many of these Jews were not only pro-revolutionary but anti-Jewish. That was the condition which existed in November 1917, when one of the great movements of this or any other century took place, the Russian Revolution.

But the disillusion was not long in coming. Following World War I, during the Russian Civil War of 1919, 1920, and 1921, Jews suffered from waves of pogroms and slaughter. These were usually perpetrated by Ukrainians, who are the most notorious of Russian anti-Semites. Soviet sources place the number of Jews killed in these pogroms during those years between 180,000 and 200,000. But that was not the end of anti-Semitism.

Communist Party archives from Smolensk which have come into the hands of Western researchers tell about the peasants who grumbled about the Communist regime because it supposedly made them dependent on Jews. In the year 1922, a government commission arrived to collect the gold from the churches. The peasants threatened that if the gold were taken by force "not one Jew will survive, we will kill them all during the night." People roamed the streets of Smolensk attacking Jews, beating and screaming "beat the Jews." In 1926, the Jews were accused of, among other things, ritual murder.

The Smolensk archives are invaluable in enabling scholars to gain an understanding of the period. We learn that in factories some Jews were heckled by non-Jewish workers—they were baited, abused, beaten, and insulted and even killed. Jewish students were abused in the universities, and in Kharkov and Moscow we learn that students demanded the introduction of a quota for Jews.

Stalin's paranoid anti-Semitism toward the end of his life is too well known to require documentation. A month after his death, the "Doctors' Plot" of 1953 was officially debunked and the accused released from jail, but that enlightenment didn't last long. Under Khrushchev there was a return to anti-Semitism, not in the form of a pogrom, but in a purging of Jewish influence from all political posts both in the Soviet Union and in the satellite countries.

The most ominous shadow on the international scene today is the reemergence of Soviet anti-Semitism as exhibited in the barbarous trials which the Soviet Union has staged to intimidate and isolate its more than three million Jews. But it is not just the emergence of the anti-Semitism which is important. What is more significant is the fact that sixty-four years after the great revolution which overthrew the Czars of Russia, the nature of the anti-Semitism is almost precisely the same as that practiced under the Czars. The Mendel Beilis trial, which was a trumped-up exhibition for the purpose of satisfying the Russian masses and had international repercussions, is now mirrored by the Leningrad trials. Just as the Czars created a quota system in the universities of Czarist Russia, so the Soviet Union, today, has a rigid quota system for Jews in areas of higher education. Just as the *Protocols of Zion* tried to prove the existence of an international Jewish conspiracy, so in all of the Soviet press today there is the assertion that Jews and "Zionists" are the invisible power which controls the great Western nations, international press, and business. Just as Jews during the middle of the nineteenth century and the early years of the twentieth century tried to escape from Czarist Russia and were punished if caught, so today Jews are trying to escape from the Soviet Union and are punished if caught. Perhaps the only difference is that the punishment is even harsher today than it was under the Czars.

The Czars are laughing because the Soviet Union in its treatment of Jews has remained steadfast to the ideals which pervaded Czarist Russia. The Czars are also laughing at the Jews themselves. They are laughing at those Jews who believed that one could substitute a social and economic system for four thousand years of religious tradition.

The two are not mutually exclusive. One can be a believer in social justice, economic equality, and personal liberty and still live as a Jew. Perhaps, nothing has been quite as pathetic in my own intellectual experience as those young Jewish men and women who, when I was at college, swore undying allegiance to the Soviet Union and called it "the new paradise for the workers of the world," and then in 1939 found that the leaders of this paradise had merged with the leaders of the greatest hell on earth the world has ever known. The Stalin-Hitler pact broke the hearts and backs of those people who had given so much to their beliefs in social justice.

I wish I could say that they all learned their lesson, but it is not true. At this very moment there are Jewish students on the college campuses of the United States, and in other areas of life, who have jettisoned their beliefs as Jews—who have become, in fact, anti-Zionists—in their attempt to fight for what they consider social justice.

The fact that elements in the Black Panther movement utilize the propaganda of the Arab terrorists and are supplied with money as well as material by the same source, the fact that the Arabs are being assisted by the Soviet Union, which has proved itself to be anti-Semitic and a nonbeliever in the equality of mankind, the fact that Islamic nations have in the last two years slaughtered thousands of Blacks in nations of Africa—all of these facts have been ignored in the wild attempt to seek an identity outside of Judaism.

I will not chase after these young people. I am one who does not believe in trying to win them back. We will not have to. As in 1939, they will be disillusioned, and I do not want to be a party to the disillusionment. I want those in whom they believe to do it themselves, and most assuredly they will.

So, the Czars are laughing. The Czars are laughing at the Russian peasant who now is a Russian worker with about as much privilege as he had before. Whose clothes are a little bit better, whose food is, perhaps, a little more plentiful, but whose basic right to exist as a human being, whose basic right to think independently, is very little better now than it was then. And the Czars are laughing at those Jews who helped to overthrow the

Czars in the hope and belief that they were escaping from their prison. They did not escape from the prison, they simply changed the keepers of the prison.

However, there is one encouraging note. The Jews of the Soviet Union are frightened, as assuredly you and I would be, but they are not succumbing to their fright. They are fighting for the right to emigrate, they are fighting for the right to identify themselves as Jews. Further, the international Jewish community and, the international community of decent people are all lending their voices and strength to achieving a victory in their struggle. I believe firmly that this time we will prevail.

The Jewish Defense League: An Appraisal

In discussing the Jewish Defense League we are faced with the problem of overcoming emotional overtones which exist because of judgments already reached.

Therefore let me begin by posing a question: did the Jewish Defense League arise without cause, or was there a particular problem which made the League an acceptable organization at the time of origin? For some years now, the problem of the Jews in the inner city has plagued the Jewish community. These are predominately elderly Jewish people who have been living in sections of New York City such as Crown Heights, the East Bronx, the Tremont area, and the Hunts Point area for many, many years. They are living in rent-controlled buildings or have small businesses, and they cannot afford to move. These elderly people cannot find housing to fit their pocketbooks. They are not anxious to be on welfare, and the traumatic experience of leaving a neighborhood where they have lived for as many as thirty or forty years simply cannot be faced. This is true not only in New York but in Boston, Philadelphia, and in other major cities of the country. However, living in these sections presents certain hazards. For example, a survey recently taken of four hundred Jewish families living in the Tremont Avenue area of the Bronx indicated that members of these four hundred families were mugged on the average of three times a year. They cannot go out in the evening. When the sun goes down, they lock themselves in their apartments, double-bolt the doors, and are imprisoned from sundown to sunup.

When the Jewish Defense League first came into existence, its purpose was to protect Jews and Jewish institutions in these neighborhoods. The problem which the Jewish Defense League sought to solve was not an artificial problem—it was a real problem which needed a solution, and no one within the Jewish community was doing anything to solve this problem.

Therefore, it must be admitted at the outset that there was a vacuum within the Jewish community with reference to the Jews in the inner city, and the Jewish Defense League tried to fill this vacuum. There was precedent for this in some areas. Defense groups had been formed as police auxiliary groups to escort people from the subways to their homes, or from the synagogues to their homes, and the need for this kind of assistance, disgraceful as it may be, was nevertheless real and pressing. Because there was a problem and because the Jewish Defense League claimed that it had been created to solve the problem, there were many Jews who accepted the existence of the Jewish Defense League and contributed to its support.

The drama of this organization did not last very long. The public becomes quite blasé even about the most traumatic of situations. The Jewish Defense League was led by a man who was not an outstanding leader in the community. His budget was minimal, his claims always were larger than his results, and the very nature of the organization demanded that it attempt to capture the attention of the Jewish community in one sensational manner or another in order to keep its coffers filled.

The problem of Soviet Jewry also is a real problem. Thus again, I must point out that we are not dealing with an ephemeral problem, but with reality. The problem of Soviet Jewry, although of great interest to all Jewry, for a time did not occupy center-stage in the thinking of our community. The problems of Israel, the Six-Day War, the threat of renewed warfare by the Egyptians, the terrorist activities on the borders of Israel, were all factors which seemed to be of greater immediate importance than the fate of the more than three million Jews in the Soviet Union.

The Jews, by nature, are not a terrorism-oriented community. We have lived too long, we have been civilized for too many years, and our experience is far too great to allow us to indulge in violence, which in the last analysis gains attention but solves no problem. Therefore when terrorism was practiced by the Arab hijackers, when El Al offices were bombed, there was a great deal of head-shaking and resolution-passing, but little else. The world community and the governments of the world community were not going to involve themselves in any kind of actions which would embarrass them to any degree. It did not seem important enough to create international tension.

Undoubtedly, there was a growing awareness of Soviet Jewry's need for help, but that help was slow in coming, and the process was being conducted with the politeness and reserve of the diplomatic corps. The Jewish Defense League once again saw a vacuum it could fill, and so it created the slogan "Never again!" Now, this slogan was a stroke of genius, for it caught the imagination of almost all Jews. Is there any Jew in the world who would deny the justice of the cry "Never again"? Thus, because we approved of the slogan, we were drawn into the trap of approving the means of implementing the slogan. Had any other organization found the same slogan before the Jewish Defense League, had any other group come to the fore for the purpose of casting light on the tragic situation of Soviet Jewry, I am sure that the Jewish Defense League would never have achieved its position. But no one did, and therefore the Jewish Defense League found fertile ground and was able to capture the front pages of the newspapers of the world.

No single Jew in the last twenty years has received the publicity that has been received by Meir Kahane, the head of the Jewish Defense League. When the *New York Times* devoted not only a front-page story but almost a full page to his career and his program, the eyes and ears of the world were focused on this man. All of us disapprove of the violence practiced against Soviet consulates, airline offices, cultural exchange programs, yet nowhere, and at no time, was the problem of Soviet Jewry so thoroughly aired and given such publicity.

A short time ago, David Susskind presented two sides of the Jewish Defense League controversy. He devoted the first half of his program to members of the League and the second half to members of the established Jewish organizations who deplored the actions of the League. Now, it is quite true that Rabbi Kahane in his presentation indicated a kind of mentality which charitably could be called neurotic, but he had on the program with him a young Russian Israeli who said something that struck home very strongly. This young Russian, who had migrated to Israel, said that on two previous occasions he had come to this country and had attempted to interest the Jewish community in the plight of his brethren in the Soviet Union. At no time was he able to achieve this. "Tonight," said he, "I am here on the David Susskind show." "This," he said, "was due not to anyone else's effort, but the Jewish Defense League. Were it not for the Jewish Defense League, as evidenced by the fact that I am appearing with members of the League, I would not have been asked."

The opponents of the League then appeared. Though some of them are close friends and colleagues of mine, I must confess that I was not at all satisfied with their presentation of the anti–Jewish Defense League position. Their condemnation was too general, too fulsome, and they did not once admit that perhaps the reality, the seriousness, the catastrophic proportions of the problem of Soviet Jewry had helped create a situation which could be one of the causes for the rise of the Jewish Defense League. It could have been said, without apology, that the Jewish Defense League had served its purpose, and now that it had brought the plight of Soviet Jewry to the attention of the world, a new procedure had to be found to solve the problems which now are universally acknowledged.

Instead, there was wholesale condemnation of the League. I do not, in any way, condone violence, but I also do not condone nonviolence which results in the destruction of a community of three million people. The various organizations which were involved on that television show had areas of interest other than Soviet Jewry. One organization was represented by an individual whose prime interest is ecumenical, the bringing together of various religious groups and the elimination of religious anti-Semitism. That is good and necessary, and no one is opposed to it. Another group that was represented is one that struggles for the civil rights of Jews in this country; it has fought throughout the years against the economic boycott of the State of Israel and has done invaluable work in many, many fields, but Soviet Jewry was not one of its principal targets.

In making any appraisal of the Jewish Defense League, it must be said that it dealt with a problem which for a time was not given sufficient attention by other Jewish organizations. This, however, does not excuse the continuation of the League's procedures, nor does it condone the League's abuse of the acceptance it won among Jews, who appreciated the concern for Soviet Jewry and were interested in assisting in its fight for survival.

The situation is similar to the struggle which took place in the State of Israel when that state was created. The state had its army, and that army was under the control of the civil government and responsible to that government. The terrorist groups, which had served a purpose in pre-independent Israel, attempted to continue their existence. This could not be allowed. You cannot have an established, responsible state which condones or accepts the existence of terrorist groups. They were asked to disband. When they did not disband, they were outlawed.

I believe that the same situation exists at this time. The Jewish Defense League served a purpose. Anyone who denies this is not facing the facts. But after it served its purpose, it was duty bound to bow out and to refrain from continuing a type of conduct which is no longer acceptable or helpful, now that the purpose for which it had been initiated has been achieved. There is a time and place for everything, and the Jewish Defense League refuses to recognize that it has outlived its time and purpose.

But unlike many others, I do not condemn the Jewish Defense League in wholesale fashion. Rabbinical associations, congregational associations, have all passed resolutions condemning the League. The State of Israel has suggested that the program of the Jewish Defense League will only lead to harm. There is a difference between the criticism by the State of Israel and that by some of our American Jewish organizations. The State of Israel did not condemn the League out of hand; it condemned further activities by the League and called such activities harmful. It did not say that the League should never have come into existence; it did not say that it had not served a purpose. Other organizations have been far less generous. The slogan "Never again" is one which we can well remember. The problems which the Jewish Defense League faced are still real and pressing. If we do not want the Jewish Defense League to continue with this type of action, then we must take action where these same problems exist. We cannot condemn and not offer an alternative.

The American Jewish community should do something far more important and far more constructive than condemnation. It should initiate and maintain a program of action in behalf of Soviet Jewry which will make unnecessary any further activity by the Jewish Defense League or any other organization which utilizes terror and violence. These are not traditionally Jewish actions. On the other hand, the Israeli wars in 1948, 1956, 1967, and 1973 were not traditionally Jewish. The need to survive outweighs tradition, and for over three million Soviet Jews the question is one of life or death. In the face of this, we cannot spend time berating each other. Let us, rather, concentrate our efforts on the principal objective—the salvation and safety of Soviet Jewry.